9/16/2

For my Fri.... ......

Thank you for your friendship and

thank you for your service —

I hope you enjoy my story —

Joe Rhodes

FLY IT HOME

Letters From Nam

Joe Rhodes

Order this book online at www.trafford.com
or email orders@trafford.com

Most Trafford titles are also available at major online book retailers.

Printed in the United States of America.

ISBN: 978-1-4907-3371-5 (sc)
ISBN: 978-1-4907-3372-2 (hc)
ISBN: 978-1-4907-3370-8 (e)

Library of Congress Control Number: 2014907007

Trafford rev. 04/14/2014

 www.trafford.com

North America & international
toll-free: 1 888 232 4444 (USA & Canada)
fax: 812 355 4082

PREFACE

The drafting of this book is an actual chronological "diary" which I penned and sent home from the war zone of Vietnam. Some entries are just pieces of letters which yield actual war information, while others are entire letters expressing thoughts of being ten thousand miles from home. I got to spend my entire year of deployment from August 13, 1970, through August 12, 1971, in-country.

The title I chose for this collection of memories also involved the letters that I wrote to my family back home. Above the address area of the "airmail" envelopes that I used to mail letters in, I would diagonally print, "Fly It Home." Since that phrase seemed to be a common thread of the letters, I decided to use that as the title for this book.

This collection is not a book of heroic actions but one of a soldier doing his duty for his country.

"Be a good soldier."

The first letter of my Vietnam experience was one penned by my mother, Bessie Alice Scriber Rhodes. There were born to Bessie Alice and George W. Rhodes seven sons. There were no sisters in my nuclear family, and I am the baby of the bunch, the seventh son. Every son served our country in uniform; Rex, the oldest, served in the Army and was a Paratrooper, having bailed out of helicopters at Fort Benning, Georgia, before being discharged from the Army on a hardship discharge. Rex was married, and he and Emily were parents to two young children who needed their daddy worse than the Army needed him because his service occurred during peacetime in our country. Ross, the second born, spent six years in the Louisiana National Guard, earning an honorable discharge. Ray, the third son born, also spent six years in the Louisiana National Guard, earning an honorable discharge. Fred, son number four, served three years on active duty in the Army. He spent thirteen months in South Korea and earned an honorable discharge. Paul, the fifth son, joined the U.S. Navy and sailed on two destroyers as an electrician's mate. The USS *DeHaven*, DD-727, often sailed close enough to Hai Phong Harbor in the South China Sea to bombard Hanoi with its big guns. The *DeHaven* spent many days in the South China Sea, delivering firepower to help the troops who were inland. After four years, Paul was rotated out of the Navy with an honorable discharge. Tommy, son number six, joined the U.S. Marine Corps, learned how to work as a plane captain for the VMO-2 Squadron, stationed at the Fifteenth Aerial Port in DaNang. Tommy had to have permission to join the Marine Corps from the Commandant of the Corps due to the fact that Tommy only measured about five feet four inches tall, weighing about one hundred and two pounds, soaking wet. But Tommy's heart and soul poured into the Corps for four years, and he was honorably discharged after attaining the rank of sergeant. The next one that Momma and Daddy sent off to war was me, the seventh son. I served in the 282nd Assault Helicopter Company, headquartered at the Marble Mountain Air Facility, which is on the beach at DaNang. After a year at Marble Mountain, I had a change in duty station and wound up at Fort Carson, Colorado, for the rest of my service. All seven sons served our country in its time of need. We were not "heroes"; we were just doing the duty which our country asked that we do.

So, as you might understand, Momma got to be pretty good at writing each of us a farewell letter. The following was written to me the night before I was scheduled to report to Fort Ord for a plane ride to the war zone of South Vietnam.

Good-bye, Sweet boy—have a good trip and be a good boy. Remember the things Momma and Daddy have tried to teach you down through the years.

I will be thinking about you every hour in the day. Write often, and be a good soldier.

Signed—Your Devoted Mother

That letter went with me to Vietnam, and it also came back with me, and now it is in a frame that houses my honorable discharge, my boot camp picture, a 282nd AHC patch, and a picture of my momma in the center of the frame.

After boot camp, I was stationed at Fort Eustis, Virginia, for Advanced Individual Training. After learning how to work on airframe repair, I was supposed to receive orders to go to Fort Hood in Texas to learn how to fly helicopters. My printed orders indicated that I was to report to Fort Ord, California, to be shipped to Vietnam. I visited with my CO, and he told me that I needed to cover this with the Adjutant General's Office and get my orders corrected. I followed his instruction on three occasions, and I kept getting orders to go to Vietnam. After much aggravation, I agreed with the Adjutant General's Office to proceed to Vietnam. One more problem had to be dealt with. I had a brother, Tommy, already in-country, so the only way I could implement the orders was by signing a waiver of going to Vietnam over choosing a base in the continental United States. In other words, I wound up volunteering to go to Vietnam. I arrived in-country at Bien Hoa Airbase, not far from Saigon. After a week there, orders came to me which would assign me to an Assault Helicopter Company, on the beach at DaNang! My first thought was that I would get to spend some of my tour with my brother, Tommy. So for my first five months and Tommy's last five months in-country, we got to visit each other fairly often, which was always a welcome visit. So . . . we visited when we could, fought when we had to, and were always on our toes.

ACKNOWLEDGMENTS

I would like to acknowledge the following individuals for inspiring and supporting me in the efforts of using decades-old letters that I wrote home from Vietnam to tell my "story."

My dear wife, Annette, after reading a few of the letters that my mother had saved, encouraged me to write a book about my year in Vietnam. My son, Heath, and my daughters, Megan and Caley, also thought that it would be interesting to recall and write about my time there. Thanks to all three.

I would also like to thank my friend, Mary Ann Van Osdell, for her supportive role in editorial ideas, not to mention punctuation and grammatical help.

I am also appreciative of my fellow soldiers who "had my back" just as I had theirs for our year of combat. I do not know where they all are, but I can attest that wherever they are, and whatever their vocation, they all remember vividly the time they spent as members of the 282nd Assault Helicopter Company.

And of course, I would like to acknowledge my dear momma, who now walks the streets of gold with my dear daddy, for saving each letter that I wrote home during my enlistment with the United States Army.

CHAPTER ONE

So How Did I Wind Up Here?

I was born in the Deep South. I had spent my entire life in North Louisiana, living sometimes in the city and sometimes in the country. I probably enjoyed the country more than the city because there are creeks to wade across, snakes to kill, cows to feed, and even oil well derricks to climb. There is, however, a lot to be said about indoor plumbing, like everybody had in the city. In the area of North Louisiana, strong Christian values are taught to children. The Golden Rule is to be adhered to at all times: help those who need help, give to those who are in need, just do the right thing. It's the way we were raised, and we were expected to stay that way. But then, the mid-sixties came, and things started changing. Big change! So there I was . . . the youngest of seven sons, the baby brother, about to go away to college. This would be the first time that I was ever away from home for more than a week.

Then things started happening pretty fast; I moved seventy miles east of home to Ruston, Louisiana, enrolled in the Louisiana Polytechnic Institute, got a job at the Piggly Wiggly Grocery Store, secured a student loan from Ruston State Bank, pledged Kappa Sigma Fraternity (founded by General Robert E. Lee), learned how to fly small airplanes, and learned the operative definition of the phrase "party hearty." To borrow the title of one of Chuck Berry's songs, I was "Almost Grown." Or at least I tried to convince myself that I was almost grown.

I majored in Professional Aviation, which I keenly enjoyed, especially on the days that we got to fly. Ground School consisted of learning the principles of flight, FAA Rules and Regulations, meteorology, call signs, aviation terminology, rate of climb, angle of attack, carburetor heat, wing ice, stall speed, take-off speeds, landing speeds, short-field landing, downwind leg, final approach, as well as how to enter notes in the airplane logbook. Some of the things that the aviation student was required to know were quite interesting, while others were not quite so intriguing. Wing ice—what's *that*? Carburetor heat—*why*? Well, if one is flying at fifteen thousand feet, one's carburetor could freeze, and the wings could actually develop ice on the leading edge because it's a *lot* colder at fifteen thousand feet than at ground level. Meteorology was interesting. I was not aware that thunderstorms were so violent inside. There is absolutely no reason for one to fly directly into a cumulonimbus (thunderstorm) cloud. Those who have penetrated these types of clouds and lived to tell about it had stories of losing engines from the wings or even losing the wings from the fuselage of the aircraft. This turned out to be pretty deep stuff but very interesting to the student who desired to learn how to fly an airplane.

Flight school is another realm altogether. The student goes to the airport and gets a literal hands-on class about the airplane that he is about to learn to fly. In this class, you get to learn how to complete a preflight inspection of the aircraft. You get to do things like checking the propeller for any nicks or dings on the leading edge of the prop and checking the gas in the tank for any water accumulation by draining a small amount of gas from the wing tank and inspecting for any separation of gas and water. Sometimes, water vapor can accumulate in a sealed gas tank, and if so, the water will "pool" in the lowest part of the tank, which is where the check drain is located. The leading edges of the wings need to be checked for any dents. The flaps, ailerons, elevators, and rudders are moved by hand to be sure they are attached. The pitot tube, which powers the airspeed indicator in the cockpit, must be clear of debris because it operates on ram air. Then, if all is up to standard, unlock the chain that holds the plane in its parking spot, climb aboard with the instructor, and start her up! Next, radio the control tower, identify yourself and your airplane, ask for permission to take off and go to the end of the runway, rev your engine to check some gauges (while applying the brakes), and if everything checks out, put the throttle to the wall, release the brakes, and when the airspeed indicator is at takeoff speed, pull the yoke back gently, and you will become airborne. What a feeling! What a thrill! After you fly around for a couple of hours and get the "feel" of flight, the time comes to return to the airport and land your airplane on its shadow. Safely. Gently and safely. There is absolutely no need to stress the landing gear. After all, stressing the landing gear greatly stresses the instructor. And after eight to ten hours of learning how to handle the airplane with takeoff and landing and maneuvering, you get to perform your first solo flight. This is a milestone. This is a tremendous builder of confidence . . . to know that you can board the machine, start it, take off, fly to "who knows where," and bring it back down safely to its shadow. Up until the point of my first solo flight, there was no greater thrill and confidence builder in my young life than that first solo.

So there I was, away from home, having a little spending money and access to one of my brothers' cars, in a fraternity, watching Terry Bradshaw quarterback our Bulldogs—yes, *that* Terry Bradshaw—learned how to drink beer, and, in short, discovered exactly how to, as some of my Cajun friends would say, "pass a good time." So started my college education, one that would be interrupted by a trip that would take me much further than seventy miles from home.

The world, however, kept spinning, and things other than what I primarily had an interest in kept spinning with it. Music of the sixties changed the ideas many people had and also the manner in which they expressed themselves. Politics also changed the outlook that people proclaimed. There was Woodstock, Janis Joplin, Jimi

Hendrix, and many other artists who gave people ideas about how the world was changing. And it changed. Rowan and Martin's "Laugh In," was a stretch to watch in many of the homes in the Bible Belt. There were go-go dancers who were good at go-going. There was something called "free love." Being a son of the Heart of Dixie, I am not sure that I ever really learned exactly what that meant. And of course, "Make love, not war" was a popular proclamation. So within a year of my first solo flight of an airplane, the U.S. Army convinced me that in all actuality, we, in fact, needed to make more war and apparently less love. Thus came my introduction to the Army of the United States of America and my duty to serve the country that affords us the freedoms that I had grown up knowing were the best freedoms that the world had to offer. So after the Department of Defense reactivated the Draft Lottery, I took it upon myself to chat it up with an Armed Forces Recruiter. I talked to the Navy Recruiter first, but enlistments in the Navy were for four years, and I just didn't want to be away from my roots for that long. Then I met with the Army Recruiter, and he actually painted quite a nice picture that I considered to be beneficial to me and my country. Since my draft lottery number, which was based on birthdates, was forty-seven, I felt that I would be drafted within just a few months.

The expectations that my recruiter said were pretty standardized were: 1) I was eighteen years old, 2) I had some college time, and 3) I could fly an airplane. If I were to wait and probably be drafted, I would very likely wind up in the infantry. On the other hand, if I volunteered to join the Army for a three-year enlistment, I would very likely wind up in Army Aviation, possibly even going through Army Flight School and becoming a helicopter pilot. Even though flying a rotory—wing aircraft wasn't my desire, compared to carrying a forty-five pound M60 Machine Gun with ammo draped over my shoulder, on the ground, helicopters started singing a real nice song to me. A short time later, after a swearing-in ceremony, I was bussed off to Fort Polk, Louisiana, to begin my duty payment for being an American. It has been said that whenever an individual takes the oath of enlistment into the

Armed Forces of the United States, that person, by taking the oath, signs a "blank check payable to the United States in the amount up to and including his or her life." This is not just a cliché. There have been recorded 641,800 combat-related deaths involving our military machines since the Revolutionary War. When the Civil War mortal casualties are included, that number rises to 1,264,826 deaths of Armed Forces personnel. So the threat of paying the ultimate price for defending freedom within our borders and around the world plays a very real part in the life of our Armed Forces personnel.

Boot camp . . . here I come!

CHAPTER TWO

Fort Polk, Louisiana

Fort Eustis, Virginia

United States Army Training Center Infantry, First Training Brigade, First Battalion, Company C. That's the "drawn out" name of our training outfit at Fort Polk. We came to be known simply as "C-1-1" when identifying ourselves to any observing trainers. "You've seen the rest, now see the best! C-1-1, Drill Sergeant!" This was much easier to say or even remember when describing to someone the company to which you belonged.

Boot Camp, surprisingly, was not as bad as some might describe. The primary thing to remember in boot camp is that you are the student, and the drill sergeants are the teachers. It seems that drill sergeants are aptly named. They "drill" into the recruits the things that can save a soldier's life on the battlefield. It isn't feasible that they could teach lifesaving or life-sustaining tactics through suggestive ideas or reading. Consequently, they are called "drill sergeants" instead of "suggestive sergeants." I believe that I speak for literally millions of Armed Forces personnel when I proclaim that the training that is received in boot camp is better learned from a drill sergeant than from a suggestive sergeant. The term of the decade, "politically correct," has absolutely no place in the Armed Forces training facilities known as boot camp. The drill sergeants, also known as drill instructors, or DIs, do not ask much of the recruits under their charge. In fact, I don't think they *ask* anything of the recruits; they *demand* from the recruits. They demand and expect the complete best from the recruits whom they teach because the DIs know that the very recruits that are under their charge will likely be in a life-threatening situation before their enlistment time is over. Consequently, the DIs grow to know their recruits quite well because they know that the things the recruits take away from boot camp are the things that could ultimately save the soldiers' lives and concurrently the life of our country. When I served, the U.S. Army Boot Camp was only eight weeks in duration. There is a tremendous amount of learning in that short eight weeks. Recruits become soldiers in that time. They learn what infantry is all about. The infantry part of our Army is comprised of the soldiers on the ground, leading the fight, looking the enemy in the eye, and carrying out the orders of their commanders to win the battles of engagement, usually with arms, i.e., rifles, grenades, and mortars. The commanders may be the one's calling the shots, but the infantrymen are the ones who pull the triggers and the grenade pins. I will not go into detail about all that is taught in Boot Camp, but some of the "blocks" of training are Rifle Training, Bayonet Training, Grenade Training, Quick Kill Training, Confidence Course Training, Close Combat Training, CBR (gas chamber) Training, Infiltration Training, just to name a few. In each of the blocks of training, the trainee either passes or fails and has to repeat the failed parts. There's no such thing as grades; it's just pass or fail. My class began on February 9, 1970, and Graduation Day was April 3, 1970. Speaking only for myself, Boot Camp was not a "cakewalk," but it could have been much worse. As long as the recruit does what he is ordered and to the expectations of the DI, usually, there is a feeling of accomplishment and growth. Boot camp, in general, starts the recruit on the road to becoming a true soldier, a servant of the United States, and a very welcome sight to those who need help in keeping their way of life that they desire.

Upon graduation from Boot Camp, the next training that the soldier encounters is called "Advanced Individual Training" or, as the Army calls it, "AIT." AIT provides the training that the soldier will specialize in while being in the service. As one can imagine, the Army must have specialists in just about any occupational field known to mankind. The Army is self-sustaining in everything from the cradle to the grave. Literally. The United States Army can stand on its own as a nationality or group of populace. To be self-sustaining, however, soldiers must be trained in the specialties that are much like links in a chain. Each specialty, or job, represents a link in the chain. That is why AIT is such an important a part of each soldier's training. After a week-long furlough at home upon graduation from boot camp, I was sent to Fort Eustis, Virginia, for my advanced training. My Military Occupational Specialty, or as the Army calls it, MOS, was coded as "68G20," which is defined as airframe repair. I believe that it was probably someone from the Department of Defense who, somehow, determined that the code name for Airframe Repair School should be 68G20. I have been unable to connect the dots that would explain the reasoning behind the code. Fortunately, it was not required that I be able to crack that code.

In Airframe Repair School, the trainee learns how to repair aircraft skin and supporting frames that have been damaged due to natural wear and tear as well as damage from unnatural sources such as bullet holes from the enemy trying to shoot down the aircraft. Most of the world's aircrafts are built of aluminum. Aluminum is the metal of choice for framing, bulkheads, and skin because the physical properties of aluminum are conducive for flying machines. Aluminum is strong, rigid, pliable, easy to bend and drill, and is inexpensive compared to other metals. Aluminum is also the metal of choice for most flying machines because it is very light in weight compared to other metals. The 68G20 trainee learns how to repair any damage to an aircraft that is repairable. For example, if a helicopter is on a combat mission and takes on small-arms fire from the enemy but is still airworthy, the 68G20 graduate knows how to assess the damage and repair the aircraft with the proper equipment, parts, and tools. Conversely, if a helicopter is shot down and completely demolished in the crash, the 68G20 graduate would not be able to repair such a calamity. In such a situation, the lives of the crewmembers are what count. Replacement helicopters can be requested from the DOD, but if a crewmember or an entire crew is lost, that becomes the most important casualty of a conflict. Being a veteran of an Assault Helicopter Company which was engaged in combat, I have witnessed both of the aforementioned situations.

After learning how to work on aircrafts and graduating from AIT, my next assignment wrought much confusion due to the difference between what I expected from the Army and what the Army expected from me. Allow me to "splain, Lucy." During my training at Fort Eustis, there was a time that I was asked by one of the company's officers if I was interested in pursuing Army Flight School since I had already had some flight training in college. I indicated that I was highly interested in attending Flight Training. I submitted to a flight physical, which I passed easily because at nineteen years of age, my hearing and eyesight were perfect, and I had no health problems that would keep me from becoming a pilot in the Army. Graduation from AIT came in early July 1970, and orders were processed for each soldier's next duty station. I was a bit surprised and a bit discouraged when I received my orders for my next Duty Station because I was expecting to be receiving orders to attend Army Flight School. The orders that I received stated that I was to report to U.S. Army Overseas Replacement Station OAB, Oakland, CA, on August 9, 1970, for transport to Vietnam for my next Duty Station. My first reaction was one of confusion and near amusement; I thought, *These orders aren't right. I'm supposed to go to Flight School.* I took the orders to the company commander's office and talked to some officer of authority, and he told me that it appeared that the orders were, in fact, invalid due to the assumption that I was to attend Flight School. He advised me to take a copy to the Adjutant General's Office and let them know that there was a mistake in my orders, and they would issue new, corrected orders. So off to the AG's Office for my ticket to Flight School I went. I met with a First Lieutenant from the Women's Army Corps who told me that she could correct the change of Duty Station and have my new orders in about two days. A couple of days passed, and just like she told me, my new orders were delivered. Another problem came along with the new orders. The "new" orders were the exact same orders that I had received three days earlier, stating that I was to report to OAB, Oakland, CA, for overseas replacement in Vietnam. Not wanting to give up the opportunity to go to Flight School, I visited with the AG's Office again and the same Assistant AG that tried to help me the first time said that she did not know why the same orders were generated. She told me to go back to my quarters and await new orders which would be arriving in a couple of days. I went back to my barracks, which were empty because all of my classmates had gone on to their next duty station or had gone home on leave, and waited for the "new" orders. Two days later, I received the same orders as before, no changes made. By this time, I had become quite familiar with the AG's personnel, and when the third set of orders came to me with absolutely no changes, I visited with the AG's folks and told them that I would just go ahead and accept the orders as they were because it appeared that they were not going to change. At this point, I was told that I would be required to sign a waiver requesting to serve in Vietnam rather than at any duty station in the continental United States because I had a brother who was a Marine presently stationed in Vietnam. This meant that for me to go to Vietnam, I had to volunteer to go. The lieutenant typed the statement declaring that coercion had not been used to get the voluntary statement from me, and I signed the statement and caught the next flight from Newport News, Virginia, to Shreveport, Louisiana, for my short leave before reporting to OAB in Oakland, California, for transport to Vietnam on August 9, 1970. There were four days of processing to be completed before I boarded a DC-8 along with about a hundred and fifty more soldiers on August 13, 1970, with a destination of Bin Hoa Air Base, Republic of South Vietnam. The show was over, and we left the building, much in the style of Elvis.

CHAPTER THREE

Letters to Fly Home

"Dear Folks"

During the last half of the month of August 1970, I wrote at least six letters to Momma and Daddy. There was some excitement in some, and others were just the cursory: *Not much going on here. How's everything there?* Of course, there was always the threat that "Charlie" could launch an attack at anytime, 24-7, but most of the assaults on our compound usually occurred in the middle of the night from about 0100 hours to 0500 hours. On nights that were clear and the moon was out, we rested better than on nights that were overcast with clouds because on a clear, moonlit night, mortars and rockets leave a very clear condensation trail that would lead to the exact location from which the mortar or rocket was launched. With a condensation trail to follow, the pilot of a gunship can easily hunt down "Charlie's" location and arrange a meeting with "Charlie" and his Maker in the matter of a very short time. Suffice it to say that we preferred the clear, moonlit nights.

On August 24, 1970, I wrote a letter to Momma and Daddy, letting them know that everything was okay at Marble Mountain, at least for the moment. August 24 was on a Monday, and on the previous Saturday morning, a little boy was accidentally struck by

11

an Army truck, and the child did not survive. There were quite a few VC sympathizers in the DaNang, area and there were plenty of actual VC there as well. When a child is harmed or killed due to the actions of the U.S. Forces, the residents and NVA in the area try to show more activity against any and all U.S. Installations. "Charlie" really tries to flex his activities in harming any and all U.S. Forces or U.S. hardware, like aircraft, tanks, etc. On the Marine side of our compound, a booby trap was set off in a toilet, and later on the same day, a guard was shot by the VC. There were several VC that were captured around the perimeter of Marble Mountain and held and interrogated. Two of the VC talked and confided that our compound was to get rockets and mortars that night, but due to the number of gunships that we had launched to patrol around Marble Mountain, there was not a shot, mortar, or rocket fired. Quite a few flares were launched over the area, and these types of flares will light up a large area almost like the crack of dawn. It turned out to be a calm night, and it was also calm on the night of August 25 due to the amount of flight activity in our area.

I wrote another letter home on August 25 and reported that another child was run over by another truck. Consequently, we could not leave the compound due to the fact that if a U.S. soldier was seen in the area, there stood a very good possibility that he would be shot by a sympathizer or an NVA Soldier. That was about all the news around Marble Mountain for that letter. I did mention, however, that we had an inspection by a colonel. The inspection went well, and our company commander was happy because that inspection probably meant a promotion for him. I closed out the letter with my salutation of "Love, Joe" and added a postscript that said that I have 352 days left in Vietnam.

CHAPTER FOUR

Good Morning, Vietnam

All right! My permanent Duty Station, the 282nd Assault Helicopter Company, home to the "Black Cats" and the "Alley Cats." By the time I arrived in August 1970, our company was known as the Black Cats. We flew Huey UH-1s, B, C, and H models. The B and C models were the gunships, loaded with miniguns, door guns, and rocket pods on each side of the helicopter. "Charlie" didn't walk away after a fight with one of the Black Cat gunships. The door gunners have an M60 Machine Gun on each side, the miniguns have five rotating barrels on each side and are capable of firing about seven thousand rounds per minute, and there are rocket pods that house up to seventeen rockets on each side. This is a force to be reckoned with. One can discern the sound of the M60 with very short gaps between each round being shot. The miniguns are Gatling Gun-style arms that, when firing, sounds like a very loud *humm*. And the rockets, well, they sound like exceedingly large bottle rockets that one buys at a fireworks stand when they leave the pod. Upon impact, however, they make an exceedingly loud *ka-boom* sound that wipes out everything in a specified area, and the rockets can also blow up other aircraft, tanks, troop carriers, and other crafts of transport. When our helicopters would launch into a mission, regardless of day or night, there was always the possibility that they would receive hostile fire, and quite regularly after returning to Marble Mountain, the crew chief of the ship would closely inspect all areas of the ship to determine if it had received any hostile fire. If there was damage by rifle fire or shrapnel, the ship would be moved into a maintenance hangar to be repaired. This is where I would perform my work. I was trained to repair damage caused by small-arms fire or shrapnel damage. As one might imagine, a fairly slow-moving target with lots of surface area flying in a war zone usually gets shot at very often. Sometimes, the bullets hit the craft and sometimes not. When there are bullet holes in the ship, they have to be repaired so the craft can maintain its airworthiness.

For about the first three or four days at my new permanent Duty Station, I was taken to all parts of our facility. I was taken to my living quarters first so I could unload and put away my gear. Thus far in my Army career, I had resided in barracks. Now things were a little different. There were no barracks at Marble Mountain. We all resided in "hooches" that served as home to about twelve soldiers each. Each soldier had a bed, a locker, and a footlocker. We had room for things like tape players and radios to make a sort of "home" environment. Each hooch had a protective bunker designed to protect us from mortar fire and rocket fire. Many nights, we were awakened by mortars or rockets that were fired at our base. The Viet Cong did not have GPS systems or other guidance systems for their rockets and mortars, so they might land anywhere on the base. I suppose most of the rockets and mortars were aimed at our helicopters, and sometimes they got lucky and hit one, but mostly, the rockets and mortars exploded on the landing pads or the runway, and occasionally, they would land in the living quarters.

I was given the "new guy" tour of the base. I learned where everything was—the mess hall, post office, the showers, the chapel, the medic's office, the sandwich shop, the "outhouses," the different hangars, the barbershop, and the Enlisted Men's Club. Also, we even had a recreation hall where we could play ping-pong when we felt like it. And of course, I was shown where to go to retrieve the M-16 that was assigned to me for times of guard duty or for defending our perimeter in times of a ground attack from the VC. So now that I had gotten settled in for my next twelve months living on the other side of the world, the time had come to learn about and conform to a lifestyle that was different from any lifestyle that I had previously known. After all, there I was, in a war zone, working on helicopters, armed with an assigned M-16, living in a "hooch" with a bunker, occasionally wearing a flack jacket, a steel pot (Army jargon for a helmet), assigned to guard duty for an entire month with the Marines . . . well, I was almost grown!

The first letter that I wrote home from Vietnam was penned on August 22, 1970. In that letter, I had informed Momma and Daddy that I had not yet seen my brother, Tommy. I knew that I would see him soon, but we hadn't met up with each other yet. I also told Daddy that I had made out a monthly allotment to him in the amount of $50.00 to help out around the house. Daddy had an accident in December 1961 which forced him into involuntary retirement. He had to undergo hip replacement, which left him in pain for the rest of his life. So the $50.00 allotment would come in handy to him, and I was glad that I could help. Also, the letter said that I should get promoted pretty soon, and I could probably help a little more. I even talked about setting up an allotment for a savings account, but that never came to fruition, I believe, due to my visiting the EM Club and attempting to drown my sorrows of being ten thousand miles from home. I could go to the EM Club and consume adult beverages because, as I previously stated, I was almost grown. On occasion, the EM Club provided us with a live band for entertainment. This occurred about once a month. Usually, the bands were of Asian descent, but they could play and sing quite well. It seems that the most popular song that these bands sang was "Yellow Reeber," the Asian version of Jeff Christies' hit, "Yellow River." I suppose the Asian bands were closely connected to the recording due to the popularity of China's Yellow River, the country's second longest river, eventually emptying into the Yellow Sea. I must give credit to the bands though; it was good entertainment, and the soldiers stationed at Marble Mountain were grateful for the entertainment.

In my second letter home, dated August 24, 1970, I made mention that our area at Marble Mountain *might* get hit by rockets during the night because a child was accidentally run over by an American GI driving a truck somewhere around the DaNang area. We did not receive any rocket or mortar strikes that night. Our EM Club was, however, booby trapped with a grenade that night, and supposedly, a wayward rat had somehow bumped the grenade, and the spoon released and blew the door off the club. I'm not sure how it was determined that the vermin was responsible for the triggering of the grenade. No GIs were injured. I suppose that there were bits of rat carcass found at the scene, probably with plenty of grenade shrapnel. Now that I look back on that occurrence, I don't feel too bad about the rat; it was just in the wrong place at the wrong time, but I can say with clarity that it makes me ill that the rat blew the door off our club! I believe that God put that rat there, and I am thankful for that because it could have been me or another thirsty GI opening that door. Good rat. Thank you, Lord.

I also indicated that after the grenade incident at the EM Club, we were on ground-attack alert due to the fact that one of the Marines that was on Zulu Guard, in a tower, was shot by a VC. There were several other VC on the perimeter of Marble Mountain, and after the Marine was shot, all were captured. Two of the VC gave up information saying that our facility was their target for the night for rockets and mortars, but with many flares lighting the area and several gunships airborne around our area, they decided that it was too risky to fire a rocket because the firing of a rocket or the launching of a mortar would give away their position instantly, and they would have to answer to the operational end of a gunship. And that, my friend, would be a lesson in futility. Gunships do not compromise. The operational end of a gunship is designed to facilitate the meeting of the enemy with the enemy's Maker. It's what they do.

I closed the letter by announcing that 1) I would be on Zulu Guard with the Marines next month, 2) I hadn't received any mail yet, 3) I hadn't seen Tommy yet, and 4) I had 353 days left of my battle tour. *Only* three hundred and fifty-three days! Yep, I was experiencing NGS (New Guy Syndrome). However, the last three of those four listed comments would soon change.

Holy mackerel . . . two letters in two days! I don't know how I found the wherewithal to write letters two days straight, but on August 24 *and* on August 25, I wrote letters home. Guess I felt a need to ramble on about the throes of being in a war zone. Seems that I had plans to go to DaNang Main to see my brother, Tommy, but that idea got shot down because there was another accident involving a child and an American truck, so nobody was to leave Marble Mountain by land. The only way to leave the compound was by air, and although we had a lot of helicopters airborne, I would have been *way* out of line to ask if one of them could taxi me over to DaNang Main. No can do, GI. However, one of the comments in the previous paragraph changed . . . I post-scripted my letter by announcing that now I had 352 days left of my battle tour. Ewweee . . . Time was marching on, just not seemingly very fast.

The next letter I wrote was a happy letter. I was off duty on August 26 due to pulling guard duty the night of the twenty-fifth. I reported that I slept until about noon and then watched TV for a while, went to my hangar for a little while, went to the company laundry to pick up my clean fatigues, and returned to my hooch. It was very bright outside and a little bit difficult to see in the darker hooch, so when I was walking toward my bunk area to put up my uniforms, I bumped into someone. It was only then, after literally bumping into him, that I realized that it was my brother, Tommy. That's a moment and a memory that will be with me until they put me on the other side of the grass. Reunion time! We went to see the company first sergeant to request an overnight pass to MAG-11. He granted me the pass, and Tommy and I had a real good and fun time. Tommy and two other Marines brought me back to Marble Mountain the next day, and the world seemed to get a little better, even in the war zone.

In my next letter, written on August 29, I reported that the day was a scorching 110 degrees. Hot, hot, hot. Very uncomfortable. And I was born and raised in Louisiana! I have a black belt in hot! I suppose it felt hotter than it actually was due to the fact that the South China Sea was less than a tenth of a mile from our compound. It seemed to be akin to a sauna-type atmosphere. I made note that I received my first letter from home on the day before. And that was great, to say the least. So now, I've started receiving mail, I've visited with my brother, and time is marching on . . . I post-scripted this letter with "348 days to go." *Three hundred and forty-eight days!* Time had quit marching . . . it was crawling now. But that's okay; it was my duty, and I would fulfill it.

August 31 wound up my "Fly it Home" letter-writing for my first month in Vietnam. I filled the lines of the stationery with the announcement that Zulu Guard would start on the night of September 1. This meant that I would be a Marine for a month. The duty would prove to be a learning experience. My memory is not as vivid for this month of my duty. I remember quite well that I made it through the month just fine and that I recorded my share of time in the guard towers and that in the middle of the night, the Marine Mess Detail brought around to each tower something called "Mid-rats." This was a term that I had not been exposed to in my past soldier history. I did, however, become quite fond of the ritual. Mid-rats is an abbreviated term that the Marine Corps has coined, which means "midnight rations." So in the middle of the night, the Marine Mess Detail transported out to each guard tower a meal in the middle of the night. I became quite fond of the idea and enjoyed seeing the food truck on its way to the guard towers. In fact, I was appreciative of the gesture. The food was good.

Also in the letter, I had taken notice that Momma had been putting ten-cent stamps on her letters to me, and one of the girlfriends that I left behind was using six-cent stamps on her letters to me. Consequently, I informed Momma that the mail would reach me in the same amount of time and that she could save a whopping four cents per letter. For every six letters, that would amount to a savings of one penny shy of two bits. I do not have the letters that Momma wrote to me, so I don't know if she elected to take that accounting advice or not.

Now I was already down to 346 days left of my tour. Some of those days were diamonds, and some were stones.

CHAPTER FIVE

September 1970

Guard Duty for a Month

Coordinated Universal Time (UTC) is a time standard based on International Atomic Time (TIA) with leap seconds added at irregular intervals to compensate for the Earth's slowing rotation. Leap seconds are used to allow UTC to closely track UT1, which is Mean Solar Time at the Royal Observatory, Greenwich.

Since the difference between UTC and UT1 is not allowed to exceed 0.9 seconds, if high precision is not required, the general term Universal Time (UT) may be used.

In casual use, when fractions of a second are not important, Greenwich Mean Time (GMT) can be considered equivalent UTC or UT1. Saying "GMT" often implies either UTC or UT1 when used within informal or casual contexts. In technical contexts, usage of "GMT" is avoided; the ambiguous terminology "UTC" or "UT1" is preferred.

Time zones around the world can be expressed as positive or negative offsets from UTC. UTC replaced GMT as the basis for the main reference timescale in various geographic regions beginning in January 1972.

Say what?

Allow me to 'splain, Lucy: The above is the technical, dragged-out-to-the-nth-degree, physics-professor-inspired confusing definition that is supposed to tell us what exactly "Zulu Time" means. That being said, I think about my daddy's intelligence. Daddy was a very smart person, as are my six brothers. The above banter regarding world "Mean Time," however, would not have meant very much sense to any of them. Daddy included. College Physics was one of my easier disciplines of study. I don't know why, but it just interested me a lot more than History, Government, Business Management, Sociology, or Psychology. Yet when I read the above and *try* to understand exactly how that affects me, I become confused as to what I am to glean from the words. However, our government has determined to use "Zulu Time" to define a wartime Guard Duty. The decision makers decided to name this particular shift of guard duty, "Zulu Guard." My own assertion of the definition is that Zulu Guard is guard duty that is round-the-clock duty of guarding. Forty years after I performed my duty of Zulu Guard, I can only wonder why they didn't just call it "Twenty-Four-Hour Guard." So for the month of September 1970, I was on Zulu Guard. I was in a guard tower for seventeen hours and off duty for the next day. On my "off days," I would report to my hangar and work on helicopters. Then, the next day, back to the Marine side of Marble Mountain for guard duty. It wasn't bad duty, but it was long duty. Spending seventeen hours in a guard tower, constantly watching for someone to try to climb over a fence to do dirty work, can tire one's eyes. But as I indicated earlier, the Marines fed and watered us timely, so it wasn't so bad. And besides, it was our shared d-u-t-y.

As it turned out, September 1970 was probably the busiest month of my service tour in South Vietnam. Although *everybody* was usually busy during their tours of Vietnam, it seems that I can declare that September happened to be my busiest month based on the fact that I wrote only four letters home during the entire month. Three of the four letters opened up with the words, *Well, I've only got a few minutes to write.* As I draw from memory, I was doing double duty during September. I reported in one of my letters that I was only getting about four and a half hours of sleep per twenty-four hours. The sleep time could come at just about any time of the day or night, dependent on how the seventeen hours in the tower and the day in the hangar were configured. Consequently, the month pretty much dragged by until October 1, 1970. I was happy to see October . . . finally.

I had indicated in a letter dated September 8, 1970, that my leisure time was very limited for the month. I told Momma that I probably wouldn't be writing very often until I got back to my permanent duty station in October. Visits with my brother, Tommy, would be limited as well. On a letter dated September 14, I reported that I took the opportunity to go swimming in the South China Sea. I remember swimming in the South China Sea several times during my year at Marble Mountain. It is a beautiful beach, and the water is as blue as the sky. The undertow, however, was quite strong. One probably would not really want to snorkel in the waters around DaNang due to the fact that the undertow could probably pull a swimmer out quite a bit further than a comfort zone. I did not have access to a snorkel, so I just enjoyed the cresting waves and stayed on the surface. About the only reminders that I might be in a hostile area were the guard towers, the gunships flying around, the armed guards in jeeps, and the International Red Cross ship that was anchored about a mile offshore. Omitting those reminders probably would have made me think that I was at Myrtle Beach or even Destin Beach. Oh and one other thing that couldn't be omitted was the ten-thousand-mile gap from the beach at Marble Mountain and Destin, Florida, or Myrtle Beach, South Carolina.

I penned a letter on September 16, 1970, and expressed concern about some kidney stone problems that Momma was having. She had undergone several operations for removal of kidney stones, and it seemed that she just kept cultivating more of them. Those who have experienced kidney stones declare that there probably is no greater pain to endure. Thus far, my six brothers and my daddy have never had kidney stones. I guess Momma had enough of them to make up for those that the rest of us didn't form. But as indicated, she seemed to be having trouble with them again. And this was on her and Daddy's thirty-sixth wedding anniversary. With two sons in a combat zone and some aggravating kidney stones, I suspect that this anniversary was not their happiest.

The last letter that I flew home in September was dated September 22, 1970. I stated that I had only eight more days with the Marine Corps and that I would be glad when those eight days passed. I asked about my two brothers who were back at college. Fred was in his senior year at Louisiana Tech, and Paul had enrolled at Louisiana State University, Baton Rouge. Fred's major was Professional Aviation, so I know that he was having a good time. Then there was Paul, enrolled at LSU . . . I did not know Paul's major course of study, but being enrolled at LSU, Baton Rouge, in the fall—oops, I meant during *football season*—there was a pretty good assertion that his major had something to do with Chemistry. During the fall semester, many students at LSU Baton Rouge take part in a lab experiment of breaking alcohol down into its by-products. Actually, these experiments usually occur on the weekends when the Tigers have a home game. And the Board of Governors of the LSU System does not even give credit for these experiments! If one were to "rank" this experiment on other college campuses, they would find that LSU, Baton Rouge, is the number-one campus in the entire United States for student engagement in the quest for breaking down alcohol to its other by-products. Or at least it was number one in the 1970s.

In the same letter, I asked Daddy to send me some newspaper clippings of how Terry Bradshaw was doing in Pittsburgh. I also asked him to send me clippings of how Louisiana Tech and LSU were doing as well. These are the types of things that go through the mind of a soldier who is stationed away from home. It doesn't matter if the soldier, sailor, marine, or Air Force member is in a combat zone or if they are stationed on the French Riviera; thoughts of the happenings at home will never be far from their minds. That is one of the reasons that service members keep marching and keep fighting and keep defending the thing that is closest to their hearts: home. Just one more cause to thank those service members who have endured and also those who sacrificed their lives so our nation and its people can live in freedom, with liberty and justice for all.

CHAPTER SIX

Happy Birthday, Daddy

Good-bye, Zulu Guard and Marines . . . hello 282nd Assault Helicopter Company! My home for the next eleven months, and I could live with that situation. Being on Zulu Guard for a month, serving with the Marine Corps, and living their lifestyle were probably better for me than I was thinking at the time it was happening. It is just one more thing that a combat soldier has to understand, that being, *somebody always* has to be on guard duty. If the perimeters of the compound were not guarded constantly, Charlie could march right in and probably kill or maim a lot of soldiers and equipment before he met his demise. Somebody had to pull the duty, and since we all lived and worked there, it was only fair that we all contributed our part. I was, however, very happy to get that part of my combat tour behind me.

I wrote two letters to home on October 4, 1970, because Daddy's birthday was on October 2. On October 2, 1970, I had gone to the Post Exchange over on the Marine side of Marble Mountain and bought a few things because it was the first of the month, and I had some money that seemed to be burning a hole in my jungle fatigues. Not to worry about a bad burn though; it was not a big sum of money. One of my purchases was a birthday card for Daddy's sixty-fourth birthday. When I got back to my hooch, I looked for the card and could not find it in anything that I had. So on October 4, I marched right back over to the PX and purchased another one and a book, and when I got back to my quarters, I began looking for the newer card and could not find that one either! I did, however, find that the cashier had put the second card in the book that I had purchased to keep it from getting bent in the wind being generated by our helicopters. I was glad to find it. I wrote the letter first and told Daddy what happened to the first card and that that was the reason that I didn't get it to him on his birthday. I wished for him a very happy birthday, both in the letter and the card.

Things rocked along, and I flew another letter back home on October 8. Tommy had bought Momma a ring and needed to mail it to her. His dilemma was that the Marines could go to the post office only from 11:00 a.m. until 1:00 p.m. Each time he went, the lines were pretty long, and time ran out with Tommy still in line. So he asked me if I could mail it home, and I told him that of course I would mail it. I mailed it from the Marble Mountain Post Office, and Momma had her ring within a week.

The next letter was written on October 8. In it, I told everybody that I was scheduled to be "off" on Wednesday October 7, 1970, but due to the fact that we had an MPC change, there were no Vietnamese allowed on our compound, and somebody . . . somebody had to pull KP and work in the chow hall. MPC is the government-issued money that changes periodically, and the powers that be decided that October 7 would be a good day to change to new money. After pulling KP duty in the mess hall, I was selected along with another GI from our company to guard the old money that had been turned in until a couple of army officers came to our ready room to pick it up. The total amount that we were guarding weighed in at $43,760.00, and the two officers showed up at about 1:00 a.m. to pick up the loot.

In this same letter, I told Momma that Tommy and I were going to try to call home on an international phone. The cost to us would be $42.00 for fourteen minutes of talk. That would be an exciting call if we could swing it. Tommy and I also learned that our brother, Ray, had been made a Deacon in his church, Haynes Avenue Baptist Church, in Shreveport, Louisiana. Tommy and I were very proud of him achieving that position.

The next letter that I flew home was dated October 13, 1970. Apparently Tommy had gotten a letter from Momma that said she was a little concerned about my surfing in the South China Sea. I indicated to her that she need not worry about that because it was raining, and the monsoon season was upon us, so I very likely would not be trying to surf in the rough seas that the monsoon created. And I wasn't real thrilled about being on a surfboard in the South China Sea with high winds, rain, and lightning. I can work with wind and rain, but lightning gets absolutely *all* of my attention. Although I'm b-b-b-b-bad to the bone, I can't hold a candle to a bolt of lightning!

October 15 was another letter-writing day for me. It was becoming more apparent that when I was "paroled" out of the Marine Corps and Zulu Guard, I had a lot more time to write home, and I knew that Momma needed the encouragement of getting mail from Tommy and me. At least that was a sign that we were still doing fine. Evidently, in a letter that I received from home, there was a mention of Momma and Daddy possibly moving to Dallas, Texas. I cannot recall why that would have been an option. In the letter of the fifteenth, I mentioned that I had spent the previous night with Tommy at MAG-11. We were able to get together about once a week, and I can attest that when brothers are in a combat zone at the same time and they can visit with each other occasionally, it really is a morale booster. And . . . there was talk that VMO-2 (Tommy's squadron) might move back to Marble Mountain. It didn't happen, but there was cause to hope that it might.

Sometimes, a soldier's thoughts turn to things other than being a target for the enemy or being very far from home to things like fast cars, football games, dances and concerts, baseball, hotdogs, apple pies, motorcycles, and occasionally girls. October 15 was one of those days that I must have thought about girls. I requested that Momma call a lady who lived down the street from us and get the address of her daughter who was going to Louisiana Tech. I thought very highly of this girl, and her name was Joy Lynn. Quoting directly from the letter, *I'd really like to hear from Joy. I really think a lot of her. She's a real good girl.* There was nothing amorous; I just thought very highly of Joy and would have liked to hear from her. I suppose Momma thought that all of my letter-writing should be to her and not to a high-school acquaintance because I never got Joy's college address. And in all actuality, Joy didn't attend Louisiana Tech. She attended and graduated from Cottey College in Missouri. I can understand that thought because, coincidentally, I closed this particular letter with, *It means so much to get a letter from home.* I can live with that.

Another two letters in two days came again on October 16, 1970. I went to "mail call" to see if I had any letters from home. Sometimes, in a combat zone, mail doesn't get to its destination at lightning speed. So . . . when I went to check my mail, I had five letters from Momma, all with different postmark dates on them. In one of the letters, Momma wrote that Daddy was in the hospital with hip problems again. I was hopeful that the words that I wrote in my letter would encourage Daddy to look on the bright side and that all would turn out all right. I also indicated in my letter that our area was supposed to be raked over by a typhoon. It never came ashore at DaNang, but it devastated the Philippine Islands. Even though it did not hit DaNang, we could take no chances with our helicopters, so we had to put all of them in our hangars for protection. And the next morning was a full morning of work by moving them back out into their respective designated spots.

I waited until October 19 to send my next letter home. It mentioned that Tommy managed to get a pass to visit Marble Mountain yesterday, the eighteenth. As usual, we had a good time and really were encouraged by each other when we could visit for a while. Another GI and I borrowed a truck to take him back to DaNang Main because his pass was not granted for overnight stay. We enjoyed our time together just the same.

Okay, another two days passed and two more letters written home. This letter, however, had good news in it. I received a promotion to Specialist 4th Class. I told Momma that I would now be able to send a little more money home to help out around the house. It wasn't a big raise, but I was happy to make the grade and glad to share the money with Momma and Daddy. Daddy had just undergone hip surgery, and he would be in the hospital for quite a few days, so I tried to encourage him to just take it easy while he could. I told him that Tommy and I were in very safe places, so that could be one worry that he could put aside. And I did not lie when I told him that. Of course I was referring to being in the bunker when rockets, mortars, and rifle fire started with our compound as the target. But I wouldn't have wanted Daddy to worry about whether or not one of his sons might not make it back home. Or two of his sons. So I just told him that Tommy and I were in one of the safest places in the world.

The next to the last letter of October 1970 was written on the twenty-third. In this letter, I was quite excited about a financial venture that I had read quite thoroughly about. I was thinking of buying a half acre of property on the main island in Hawaii. I learned that I could buy this land for $100.00 per month, and the property was currently selling for $4,995.00. For some very peculiar reason, I decided not to buy the property. I can only wonder how much that track of land is worth today, in 2013. If I had bought that property, I very likely could go ahead and retire from work altogether. I think I could be a real good fisherman. Or a top-notch hunter. Oh . . . the decisions we make at age nineteen. Seems like another example of being almost grown. Another pleasant surprise occurred on October 23. A very good friend of mine learned that I was stationed at Marble Mountain. He was stationed at a base with the 101st Airborne Division. His name was Randy Beckler. We were good friends in high school. We rode home from school together almost every day with Jerry Heidecker and Mike Kennedy. Mike had use of his mother's 1967 Mustang, and all four of us were real cool, driving fast and listening to the Box Tops, Wilson Picket, and Otis Redding on the eight-track tape player in the Mustang. So about ten thousand miles away from home, Randy and I got together for an afternoon of fun and catching up on what had been happening since high school. Pretty interesting conversations, to say the least! It was a really good visit for the both of us.

The last letter of October had some disheartening news to share. I was selected for Zulu Guard again for the entire month of November. This was not the kind of news that I wanted to hear. But as I've reported before, somebody had to do it, so I might as well grin and bear it. This wasn't just the Marines' war; it was ours too. So I'd go and do my duty and guard this compound against all enemies with a vengeance. December would probably bring cheer, and I would be happy to see it.

CHAPTER SEVEN

November 1970

Zulu Guard and Airframe Repair

The first letter that I flew home in November occurred on the fifth of the month. I reported to the Marine side of Marble Mountain to find out which tower I would be guarding from. Of course, they were happy to see me, and I wish I could have echoed the same sentiment, but I just couldn't muster it up. But at least it was not as bad and long as it could have been. I started my Zulu Guard assignment on November 1 and was relieved of that duty by a marine that I was very happy to see. In fact, I suppose that my replacement was the Marine Corps' birthday present to me because my replacement reported to me on November 7, my twentieth birthday! So . . . back to the Army side of the compound to do my regular job of airframe repair.

I was worried about Daddy because of the hip replacement. Time would only tell whether or not the surgery was successful. Daddy was the type of personality that you would never find loafing or not busy doing something. So this hip operation slowed him down quite a bit for about six months. Then he would occasionally use a walking cane due to arthritis pain, but he got around and did the things that he wanted to do. If the yard needed

30

to be mowed, he would mow it. If trees needed trimming, he would trim them. If the car needed to be washed, he would wash it. All, mind you, with an artificial hip. Yes, Daddy was a go-getter and was an inspiration to all who knew him.

The next letter that I sent home was written on November 23. It so happened that I had not received a letter from home in over two weeks. Very odd. I knew that something must have occurred that caused Momma not to write. Well, I learned from Tommy that Momma had been shopping in a mall in Shreveport, walked into something that had been spilled on the floor, and immediately become horizontal to the earth. Flat on her back. Momma was fifty-seven years old when she had that accident. It shook her up pretty badly. Now, here I was, trying to convince her not to worry about the accident, and I was certain that all would turn out all right. I don't know how much sincerity she read in my letter, but I was afraid that she might have fractured a hip bone or, worse yet, a vertebra. Either of those injuries can really create a lot of havoc on an elderly person. It was my prayer that she wouldn't have any future problems with a fall of that magnitude. Just another little thorn in my side compounded by the fact that I still had around 275 days left on my tour before I could go home and see if everybody was okay.

Thanksgiving Day arrived on November 26, and it was quite a different Thanksgiving than I had experienced before. I had spent the previous night with my brother and returned to my compound at around 11:00 a.m. the next day. The battalion chaplain had made arrangements with an orphanage in DaNang to let all of the children come to Marble Mountain and get to mix and mingle with the GIs from America. The children varied in age from about eighteen months to about eight years. We had a church service in the chapel, and afterward, we got to pick out a child that we could take to Thanksgiving dinner and care for until about 2:00 p.m. I picked out a real cute little boy named Hoa, and as we were leaving the chapel, I turned around momentarily to speak to a friend, and when I turned back, Hoa had disappeared. Gone . . . children were all over, but I could not find Hoa. Another soldier had taken him to the mess hall for Thanksgiving dinner. So . . . I went back in the chapel and picked out a little girl named Tai. Tai and I went outside, and she ran from me to meet up with another soldier and decided that she wanted to be with him instead of me. Thankfully, there were plenty of GIs who wanted to treat the children to dinner. It was quite a sad sight to see all of these young, innocent children who had injuries and deformations. The most gripping and sad fact was that these children had no parents. Growing up without parents is probably about the saddest experience that a child could endure.

As it turned out, this letter was four pages long. I usually sum things up in about two pages, but I was full of questions about Momma's injuries and whether or not Daddy had gotten out of the hospital. I'm certain that in the next letter that I received from home, Momma addressed those questions.

I enclosed the Thanksgiving dinner menu of our meal that the mess hall crew put on for us. We dined on turkey, cornbread dressing, and all the fixings. It was a good meal, and we were thankful to have it.

I summed the letter up with a postscript in which I requested that Momma send me nuts for Christmas. All I wanted was a variety of nuts. I asked for English walnuts, pecans, peanuts, and almonds. I do not recall exactly why I seemed to be craving nuts, but that was the case. I guess sometimes you feel like a nut and sometimes you don't.

CHAPTER EIGHT

An Odd Christmas

December 1970 proved to be a very busy month at Marble Mountain Air Facility. I do not know how many sorties the 282nd AHC flew for the month, but I am certain that it was more than for most other months. Common sense will tell us that the more a relatively slow-moving aircraft flies over known possible enemy territory, the greater is the likelihood of the aircraft receiving enemy fire. As a result, the airframe repair shop becomes much busier repairing bullet holes in many parts of the ship, including the body, the tail boom, the honeycomb floors, the plexiglass chin bubbles, the windshield, and the plexiglass skylights above the aircraft commander and the copilot seats. Some repairs take much longer to complete than others; for example, a bullet hole in the honeycomb floor takes much longer to repair than a tail boom skin bullet hole. Plexiglass chin bubbles in the nose of the helicopter usually took extra time to repair mostly due to the fact that the repair was made with fiberglass repair materials. While the repairs were being made to aircraft in our hangars, other aircrafts had to be launched into a mission to make certain that "Charlie" knew firsthand that the Black Cat Helicopter Company would continue to fly and fight all day and all night long, 24-7. It's what we were there for, it's what we did, it's what we would continue to do, and for those of us who are Black Cat Veterans, it's what we would do again if called upon. Consequently, the heavier the number of sorties flown, the busier everybody became. The busier that support personnel becomes, the less "free time" one has to write letters, visit the PX, or go to the EM Club. Due to time constraints, it appears that I only wrote one letter home during the month of December 1970. The letter was written on December 13, and the first sentence was apologetic in nature, referencing the fact that I hadn't had time lately to write a letter. Momma used to tell me when I was a child that if I didn't straighten up, she would "jerk a knot in my tail." Translated, that meant that she would pinch me real hard if I didn't straighten up and act right. I acknowledged that in my letter by telling her that I knew she could "jerk a knot in my tail for not writing." I then stated that things had been pretty hectic around the company lately. I did not tell her that our company had been flying twenty-four hours per day and that our helicopters were being shot at probably twenty of those twenty-four hours, which created a lot of work in the airframe repair shop.

I found time to include in my letter that I was having some type of dental problem. My gums in the very back of my mouth were very tender and painful. I presumed that my wisdom teeth were trying to get to the outside of my gums. After all, I was almost grown. I did not go to the dentist, and the pain eventually subsided, and as well as I can recall, my wisdom teeth stayed right where they were. I'm sure I gave them and all of my other teeth a real workout on Christmas Day. We had a traditional meal for Christmas: roasted turkey, cornbread dressing, green beans, cranberry sauce, and apple cobbler for dessert. We washed all of that down with tea. I think we all were quite appreciative of the entire mess hall crew for all that they served us.

Christmas came and went. We didn't have a Christmas tree or a visit from Santa Claus. No presents were exchanged. Presents, however, were received from home, and I can say with certainty that all soldiers assigned to the 282nd AHC was thinking of their homes and their families.

Christmas Day in 1970 was, without question, the strangest Christmas Day that I have ever experienced. Armed Forces Radio was broadcasting Christmas music all over the country, and I'm not sure that it was receptive to all who could hear it. To some soldiers, it was sad because they were not spending Christmas with their families. To me, it was just what you're supposed to listen to on Christmas, regardless of where in the world you are. Yes, we all missed being at home on Christmas, and undoubtedly, all of those at home missed their soldiers, marines, sailors, and airmen just as much. But the passing of each day meant that our deployment was one day closer to the end. And we welcomed that thought.

Our company stayed very busy during the entire Christmas and New Year season. I well remember that in school, from the first grade through college, we always had a Christmas vacation or break. In a combat zone, there is no vacation or break for any holiday. In fact, action is accelerated in combat zones during most holidays, and the combat action in and around DaNang was certainly no exception. However, our entire Armed Forces had taken an oath to defend and protect those who inhabited the regions of the globe that our nation deemed necessary for us to go to. And we meant it. We were true to our oath. Time marched on.

On January 1, we celebrated the birth of the year 1971. Although neither 1970 nor 1971 was a "leap year," to most soldiers, it seemed like we had "leap months." In all honesty, I can only speak for myself, but to me, it sure seemed like the months dragged by very slowly. We all had plenty of work to keep us busy, and normally, when one is busy, time seems to go by faster. In keeping with the proclamation that "everything is relative," I suppose the speed at which time passes is relative to one's location. Spending a year on the French Riviera would probably seem to pass faster than spending a year in a combat zone. In Vietnam, most of our deployed Armed Forces Personnel spent their *slow* year and returned home. Time, for more than 58,200 American Armed Forces Personnel, came to a stop, both for them and their families. Not all of these casualties were men. Not all women of the "Make love, not war" era wore love beads. Some wore military dog tags. And sadly, some of these women gave all they had and returned to the United States Mainland with their dog tags wrapped around their toes. Speaking personally, I cannot focus on an image of having a sister or a daughter or a mother being sent to a duty station in a combat zone. Please don't err and define me as chauvinistic in all respects. I suppose that I choose to be more protective of females than I am of other males. I believe that after Eve was given to Adam by our Creator, Adam probably was somewhat protective of Eve. In addition, I highly suspect that Joseph was protective of Mary.

By mid-January 1971, the activity that had kept us so busy during the Christmas season slowed down by a notch or two. The war was not over nor was there a cease-fire in place. We were still flying plenty of missions, and our ships were still being hit by ground fire, but it seemed that we had the time to learn some of the songs that were being broadcast by Armed Forces Radio. Hits of the day were recorded by John Lennon, who wanted to "Imagine" all manner of things, while Janis Joplin was busted flat in Baton Rouge, waitin' for a train with "Bobby McGee," and Marvin Gaye was wondering "What's Going On." Isaac Hayes was singing about a "bad to the bone" superhuman named "Shaft," as Rod Stewart was trying to get "Maggie May" off his mind, and The Rolling Stones were sweetening the airwaves with "Brown Sugar" as Carole King was "Feeling the Earth Move Under Her Feet." Ms. King was not alone feeling the earth move beneath her feet. On the nights that we received rocket and mortar fire from the VC, most of the members of the 282nd AHC, who were not airborne during the attack, felt the earth move a little as well. Sometimes, it even felt like the sky was tumbling down. Not really—I just couldn't help using Ms. King's line there.

I managed to write four letters home in January. The first one was penned on January 11, and I opened the letter with a complaint of working "pretty hard lately." I reported that I was on "standby" for the afternoon and took a shower, got in my bunk, and was asleep within about five minutes. For me to sleep in the afternoon, I must have really been exhausted. Of course, I inquired about each family member as to how everybody was getting along. Momma had her kidney stones, Daddy had his new hip, and inquiries about my brothers and their families were the norm for almost every letter that I would write. The answers were also usually about the same in the return letters.

January ended on the thirty-first, and February was ushered in. I thought things would sort of slow down after the holiday season ended. It seems that in a war zone, what one expects to happen does not necessarily occur. And actually, that really shouldn't be a surprise, especially to a participant in the war. So around Marble Mountain, we stayed pretty busy with our duties. Launch helicopters, fly the mission, fly back to the airfield, inspect the ships for damage, fix what damage there is, refuel, rearm with munitions, and launch the ship again. There just was not very much time to philosophize about the things that the deep thinkers of the past had already figured out for us. Confucius, for example, probably would not have been such a philosophical force if he had been a member of the 282nd Assault Helicopter Company in the late 60s and the early 70s. The business of war is serious though, and we probably could have used a well-grounded thinker around the hangars for something. Maybe we could have dictated our letters home for him to write, and we probably could have flown more sorties. We improvised and worked with what we had, and when we had time to write letters home, we wrote them.

It looks like I wrote four letters home in the month of February 1971. Two of them were written on the eleventh because I had already sealed the envelope with the first one, and I thought of something else that I wanted to ask Momma about. Momma's birthday was on February 18, and I was telling her that I thought I knew what she wanted and that I would be sure that she got it before I left Vietnam. I don't recall exactly what she wanted, but I suspect it was some dinnerware-like plates or silverware. I apparently thought about them wanting to buy a house that we had discussed a couple of months earlier, and the second letter of the eleventh was an inquiry about if they had made any decisions about the house. I signed the letter with a postscript that stated, *183 Days.*

Tomorrow, I start downhill—six more months and I'm home! It's a good feeling to realize that at least half of the hitch is behind, and now I was on my way out.

The next letter was dated February 23, and in it, I expressed thanks to Momma for sending me some "civvies." For those who are unaware of military terminology, "civvies" is what military members call the clothes that civilians wear. The military issued any and all types of clothing that is needed, but once in a while, it feels good to put on a pair of blue jeans and a T-shirt that is not a drab olive color. I had also commented on Daddy buying a new car. He had traded in his Rambler for a Chrysler. And I knew that he was proud of his new ride. And I was proud for him. Also in the same letter, I stated that I had received a letter from my oldest nephew, David. David had reported to me that his sister, Kaki, was getting bigger, his brother Danny was getting smarter, and his youngest brother Reagan was just a mess.

The last letter of February was written on the twenty-seventh, a Saturday. It seemed that I was full of news in this one. This is one of the few letters that I wrote that did not start with, *Well, this will be short.* At the PX at Marble Mountain, there was a way to call home, but you had to have an appointment to make the call. This was a good deed that a radio station in California was doing for military personnel and their families. The system was code named "MARS" station. I am told that MARS is an acronym for Military Air Radio Station. At your appointed time, you get to call the radio station in California and tell the "operator" what number you would like to be linked with, and they will call the final number. What is key in MARS calls is that when one party finishes talking about a subject, you have to say, "Over." Then the operator in California switches lines for the other party to talk. Momma was not used to using the word *over* when talking to someone on the phone, so the conversation went a little slow. But that was okay because it was a live link to home and family.

In this same letter of the twenty-seventh, I included an article which was published in the *Stars and Stripes* newspaper that we occasionally got. The article was about a rocket attack on DaNang

Main on the previous Sunday night. I had been on Guard Duty that night, and suddenly, the sky had gotten very bright, and just a few seconds later, I had heard the impact of three 122 mm rockets that had hit very close to where my brother's group worked and lived. Two of the rockets had impacted on the flight line, but the third had been a direct hit on a CH-130 Hercules transport turboprop. The hit had demolished the airplane. There had, however, been no airmen or marines on or around the CH-130 when it was hit. I'm sure that several gunships were launched to the suspected location of where the rockets came from, and the gunships very likely put down lots of lead as a deterrent to such foolishness. As it turned out, the CH-130 that was rocketed had been parked about a half of a mile from where my brother, Tommy, was sleeping. I'm reminded of Carole King's song about feeling the earth moving under our feet. But soon, Tommy would be scheduled to rotate back to the United States to finish up his enlistment in the USMC. Then, he wouldn't have to worry about the earth moving under his feet in the middle of the night anymore. A good thought.

CHAPTER NINE

Tommy Goes Home

Finni Marine Corps

On Monday, March 22, 1971, I got to spend the night with my brother, Tommy. I helped him pack his belongings and get everything squared away for his long flight home. The next morning, March 23, 1971, there was a chartered DC-8 parked on the tarmac at DaNang Main, waiting for the Marines to board for their anticipated flight back home to the United States of America. The charter was scheduled to depart the country at about 9:20 on the morning of March 23. Those Marines who were expected to board and go home were ready and anxious to get the show on the road. Tommy was one of them. I got to escort Tommy all the way up to the entry ladder apparatus, and we had to shake hands and say our "good-byes" at the bottom of the stairway going to the aircraft. Tommy turned and marched right up those stairs and found his seat. I walked back to the fenced area around the main terminal and watched. The engines came to life, and the big "Freedom Bird" taxied to the south end of the runway. The flight engineers and pilots performed all of the takeoff checks, revved the engines, released the brakes, and began their takeoff roll northward. About halfway down the runway, the nose lifted, and shortly thereafter, the whole jet defied gravity and took off with a nose-up attitude. There were some fairly low clouds, and as the jet penetrated the first cloud bank, the vortices circling off the wingtips were visible. I saw the jet a couple of more times flying in and out of low clouds, and soon, I did not see the aircraft again. Tommy was on his way home.

It was at this stage in my life that I think I knew that I was finally all grown up. The thoughts going through my mind were: *I'm over ten thousand miles from home; There are a large number of individuals that would like to end my life; I'm the only one in my family that is here now.* I felt all alone now that Tommy, whom I had grown up with and who had always been there for me, had left. Yes, I felt alone, but actually, things had not changed very much. I was still a member of the 282nd AHC, and there were a lot of friends and fellow soldiers that would lay their lives down to save mine, and I would do the same for them. So actually, I still had a lot of family members present, and I was not as alone as I felt while standing on the tarmac at DaNang Main on the morning that my brother and his Marine family finished their combat tour and returned home.

Although, in March 1971, the event of Tommy getting to go home was a very big deal to me, there was actually still a war going on right under our noses, so to speak. Since DaNang was the most populated city in the northern part of South Vietnam, there was plenty of reason for a member of the United States Armed Forces to be alert and, most notably, realize that there were a lot of armed people that would spend a bullet on any of us, given the opportunity. When my brother and his unit left, the VC kept up their nasty attitudes and continued to fire rockets and mortars at us when they could. In other words, it made no difference to the VC if Tommy's unit was there or not. In the business of fighting a war, it was "business as usual," which meant that our gunships and slicks were flying into hostile areas, exposing themselves to hostile fire and returning fire with a vengeance.

On the day that Tommy left Vietnam, I wrote a letter home, telling Momma and Daddy about spending the night with Tommy on his last night in-country and escorting him to the Freedom Bird that would fly him home. I was pretty quick to point out that I had only 141 days left before I too would start my journey home. I expressed hope that the next four months, two weeks, and six days would pass pretty quickly. As it turned out, the 141 days did, in fact, pass, and at that time, I started on my journey home. Other things were happening as well. I wrote in that letter that about a week before, we had launched some ships to fly north and then turn west, heading toward Laos. Our ships had been flying at an altitude of just over one hundred feet (low leveling), and suddenly, in front of our helicopters, the earth had begun exploding, in straight lines. We had been flying into a B-52 bombing run. Our pilots had begun making evasive maneuvers instantly, and none of our ships had received any shrapnel from the bombs that had been dropped from the B-52s. It's a testament to the ability of our pilots and the agility of our helicopters that no damage had been incurred to our ships or to our crews. I suspect that our pilots knew just how Jim Lovell, astronaut extraordinaire, felt when he had to radio NASA Mission Control with the comment, "Houston, we've got a problem." Whenever someone is involved on the receiving end of a B-52 bombing run, whether on the ground or in a vehicle trying to evade those bombs, that someone knows the complete and total definition of the word *problem*. I suspect, considering the "psychological factor," that some of our troops in the evasive helicopters had required assistance in removing themselves from the seats when our ships had landed on safe terrain. I, personally, cannot confirm the preceding statement, but I can say with abundant certainty that some of these soldiers had needed the assistance. That's just one more of the issues that warriors face in times of combat.

On the last day of March 1971, the VC were very active around DaNang. Actually, since the attack came in the middle of the night, I guess one would say that we were hit on April 1. The rockets were launched in waves. The first assault was on DaNang Main, and close to fifty rockets hit there; then Marble Mountain received about eight rockets, and then the rest of the rockets were launched on DaNang Main. The closest rocket to my hooch hit about twenty feet from my hooch. It was a direct hit on the hooch right across the walkway that goes between all of the hooches in our quarters. I heard the rockets start hitting the runway, and before the sirens started, I was already in my bunker. After the first rocket hit the runway, I yelled, "Hit it," code for "Incoming, get in the bunker." I threw back my mosquito netting and leaped from the end of my bunk just as the hooch next door took a direct hit. There was a very bright light from the explosion and a deafening roar. The concussion blew me into the bunker, and I landed on the floor, which was made out of 3/8-inch-thick steel, with two-inch holes punched out of the metal to give the metal more strength and rigidity. Landing and sliding on this type of flooring can cut one literally from head to toe. I looked similar to fresh ground hamburger meat, but the cuts were superficial, and I did not require medical attention nor did I seek attention for the injuries. The next morning, there was an abundance of shrapnel in our hooch. I even dug out a couple of pieces about the size of a silver dollar out of my mattress. I was lucky that I didn't get seriously wounded. Actually, nobody in our hooch got seriously hurt. In the hooch which was directly hit, there was one soldier that received mortal injuries. A couple of other soldiers in the same hooch were pretty seriously injured, but there was only one death in the barrage that Marble Mountain received that night. Out of the nearly one hundred rockets that DaNang Main received, I do not know how many injuries and casualties were inflicted. I was thankful that Tommy had already evacuated the country by a week and a half. In addition to the rockets that we received, we were also under ground attack on the south end of our airfield. The guards in the Zulu towers fought back the attacking VC before they were able to penetrate our compound in large numbers.

I started April off with a letter written on April 1, 1971. I had received two letters from home the day before and was glad to get the information that Tommy had, in fact, made it home. A short time after he left, all manner of Hades came about. There were rockets, mortars, ground attack all around Marble Mountain. There was nothing that we couldn't handle, but there was grand aggravation due to the interruption of rest times, especially at night. I'm not implying that the rest of South Vietnam was not under attack, but for some reason, the VC seemed to be ramping up their activity around DaNang. Somehow, I found time to wish that I was home with Tommy. That's not the way the Army sees it though. They, the Army, gave me a job to do, and they gave me an all-expense-paid year to do it, so that's exactly what I did. It wasn't so bad at Marble Mountain. I'm sure that the families of the fifty-eight thousand who returned back to the United States in a box would differ with me about that statement, but I categorized my comment wasn't so bad. It could have been much worse, and it was bad enough, but Marble Mountain was pretty well fortified against our enemy.

I didn't write home many letters during April. On April 8, 1971, we had three ships out on patrol, and they were shot up pretty badly. All three had to be repaired and made airworthy again, so we worked pretty late into the night to do our airframe repairs. The ships were reloaded, refueled, and rearmed, so by daybreak, they were flying again. Upon their return to the compound, they were inspected for bullet holes, and there were none on any of the three. There was quite a bit of munitions gone from the ships, so I suspect it was "payback" time for the VC.

I made note in my letter that we were served fried chicken for our evening meal. I also compared it to the fried chicken that Momma fried, and I determined that it didn't compare to Momma's fried chicken. When Momma fried chicken, it was perfect. She also complemented the meal with mashed potatoes and gravy, green beans or cabbage, cornbread, and rolls, all homemade of course.

My next letter was written on April 13. In it, I made mention that we were assigned three more civilians to our airframe repair shop. The three "new guys" would be assigned to us on a temporary basis. They were there mainly to learn how to repair airframe problems, and with the amount of work we had to do, they were a welcome sight to the soldiers who were assigned to the airframe repair shop. We were all caught up on all jobs within two weeks, and then the three new civilians moved on to other camps where their expertise could be used to make other "shot-up" airplanes or helicopters airworthy and get them back doing what they did best: stop Charlie in his tracks.

I had sent Tommy a message about going over to see his friend Dixon. Since Tommy left MAG-11, our company commander would not allow me to travel by ground through DaNang and go over to MAG-11 for a visit. Quite a few times, while Tommy was at DaNang Main, my company commander was very gracious in giving me an overnight pass to visit with my brother. That would be contingent, of course, on the workload that we had for our own helicopters. So . . . the next time that I got to go over to DaNang Main was the day that I got to start my trip home. But for the time being, I still had triple digits of days left in-country. Actually 120 days before I would change duty stations.

On Monday, April 21, 1971, I was very excited about writing my next letter. There was on our Marble Mountain Air Facility one fixed-wing aircraft group. They code named their group "The Royal Coachmen," and they flew Beechcraft King Air aircrafts. These very, very nice twin-engine airplanes were very good rides for all who got to fly in them. These folks were usually "Field Command" or "General Command" personnel who needed a flight to anywhere in the country. I don't know how many of these companies that the Army operated throughout Vietnam. But . . . one of the pilots in the Royal Coachmen knew that I had flown some in college and that I was highly interested in aircrafts, particularly fixed-wing aircrafts. He told me if I could get off on Saturday, the twenty-fourth of April, I could fly down to Tuy Hoa with him to have some radio work done on his aircraft. I managed to be off on Saturday, the twenty-fourth, and good to his word, he came to my hangar and asked if I could go with him. I affirmed with him that I could go. We (he) did the preflight inspection, filled the tanks with fuel, and went to the end of the runway. He cleared with the tower to take off, and he released the brakes, and down the runway we sped. In short order, we were airborne with the wheels up. It was a cloudy day, so we had to fly by IFR, the acronym for "Instrument

Flight Rules." In other words, we watched our dashboard of gauges until we started our descent into Tuy Hoa. Tuy Hoa is about 250 miles from Marble Mountain. We had our radio work completed, and it was time to go back to our compound. We revved the engines, and before he released the brakes, he asked me if I wanted to take it from there. Without hesitation, I told him, "Yes, sir!" The pilot released the brake and told me that the flight was mine. We zipped down the runway, and when we attained takeoff speed, I gently pulled the yoke back toward my lap. The plane took a very quick nose-up attitude. I lowered the nose so as not to stall and started trimming the wings. We climbed to an altitude of ten thousand five hundred feet and leveled off in comfortable speed and travel. Any time I hardly moved the yoke, the plane would move instantly and keep flying that way until I straightened the plane out. I haven't flown a lot of different aircrafts, but that King Air was more sensitive to moving the yoke, rudders, or ailerons than any plane that I had ever had the pleasure of piloting. We flew IFR almost all the way back. In fact, we did not stop at Marble Mountain. We flew to Phu Bai, which is probably about twenty-five miles north of DaNang. We started our decent, and just to be on the safe side, the pilot told me that he would take it in from there. That was fine with me because I am quite sure I could have hit the runway, but I just do not know how hard I would have hit it. Might have blown out a tire or two, and that would have been trouble. Regardless, it was a great day, and it's one that I'll never forget.

Also in this same letter, I announced even more news. I told Momma that the mess crew had served us fried okra a few days earlier. Of course, I mentioned to her that it hadn't been as good as hers, but that it had "resembled the taste" of southern fried okra. And it really had been very good. I told Momma that when I got home, I really wanted her to fry a big batch of okra. I feel certain that she did after I returned home. I'm fairly confident that I filled my tummy, maybe even beyond its capacity, with that meal.

The rest of the news in this letter was about a possible "early out" concerning my tour of a year in-country. There were several soldiers who were given "drops" of time which would shorten their tour. Some of them were receiving "drops" of up to forty-five days. I thought and reported that I might become the fortunate one as well as being the seventh son. I told my family that if I were to get a drop, there was a possibility that I could be home as early as July 4. I would have liked that, but it seems that the Army thought it better if I stayed right where I was assigned for the entire year. As it turned out, it looks like they were right. I was physically able to complete my duty, and I am of the opinion that I must have been there for a reason that perhaps I didn't know. Maybe my Creator had a reason, unknown to me, to be there and perform my job just like I was trained to do. I am a Fortunate One who spent the combat year in a hostile area and returned home with all of my fingers, toes, ears, eyes, and all internal organs working just fine. More than fifty-eight thousand warriors and their families were not as fortunate as I was, and I feel for those folks and their losses and in a very short time that I was, in fact, one of the fortunate ones. I am thankful for that.

April 1971 ended much like it started. There was another rocket attack on DaNang Main, and Marble Mountain was a target as well. DaNang Main received close to one hundred rockets, and Marble Mountain was hit with only about five. I believe that the damage done to our compound was miniscule when compared to the main air base. We all assumed our usual defensive positions—go to the bunkers until the rockets and mortars stop, go check out our M-16s, and ammunition and prepare for any ground attack which might follow the rocket attack. None came on this night, just the rockets and mortars. April ended, and May 1971 began. One hundred and four days left to go.

CHAPTER TEN

Patch Bullet Holes

Sunbathe
Counting Days

S ometimes, I wonder if there is a wartime duty in which one has nothing to do except reminisce about things of the past, like fun places to go, fast cars to drive, fast girls to take riding in fast cars, drive-in movies to see, backyard cookouts, and fishing or just daydream. Out of all of the different career choices that the Army offers, I don't seem to remember my recruiter mentioning a duty of this sort. I suppose that warriors wouldn't last very long if our U.S. service members had the time on their hands that the aforementioned "duty" would take. So everybody in the service has a job, and, in many cases, additional jobs, to perform. One of our forefathers, a heavy-thinking individual, made famous the cliché, "When one is busy, time goes by faster." I suppose this includes fishing, racing, theaters, barbeques, etc. However, when one is scaling fish, changing oil in their race car, cutting the grass, bathing the dog(s) and cat(s), I can assure you with certainty that time does not go by faster!

So the war extended into May 1971, and it was a lot like April 1971. Orders of the day: launch helicopters and gunships, fly sorties, return to compound, inspect for damage, repair the damage, refuel the fuel bladders, rearm all munitions on the ship, prepare for another launch. Over and over and over and over again. We became experts in this business. Although Charlie knew better than to try to mix it up with one of our slicks or gunships, he would fire lead in our direction at any perceived chance. Sometimes, his round found its target. Sometimes, he would be *seen* shooting at us. When that occurred, he was about to be sent to his next dimension on the other side of the grass. Not only was it our job, it was our sworn duty, our conscious duty, and our agreement to arrange the meeting with Charlie and his Creator. That's the order and expectation of our Armed Forces of the United States. It's not difficult to understand; there are only two endings to a war—a skirmish (fight) or an argument. These two endings are the same in any of the aforementioned degrees of disagreement: 1) Win or 2) Lose. Speaking in completely common language, the team with the greatest power and desire will win, exclusively.

In my letters home during the month of May 1971, I reported about how much work we had in the hangars. Work was so heavy that we decided to start the overnight crew hours again. I ran the airframe repair shop for the overnight crew. As well as I can recall, there was only one member on the night crew. I was the entire crew. I didn't mind being the only one in that part of the hangar though; in fact, being by myself, I could get quite a few more repairs made from 6:00 p.m. until 3:00 a.m. because I could move my equipment around in the hangar more easily than when there were more folks in the hangar performing their duties. In all actuality, the overnight shift was not that bad.

Hearing helicopters launching and landing close-by all day became like music to me. It didn't take long to learn how to sleep during the daytime hours. The sound of the rotors sounded like a sweet lullaby. Well, maybe not a lullaby, but it was the sound of safety for all inhabitants of Marble Mountain. During those daylight hours that I had to recuperate from the overnight duty, I sometimes would climb on top of our sandbag-covered bunker to sunbathe for a while. I did this so I would be looking good for when I would go home. I occasionally would take pen and paper to write a letter home from the top of the bunker. As I would write, I would also sweat on to the paper, and this would cause the pen to skip. This, coupled with the fact that I was using a sandbag as a backer for the stationery, was not conducive for good letter-writing.

Also in the month of May, we had a "new guy" move into our hooch. I think his rank was Sergeant First Class, and his last name was "Tyeskey." We all called him "Sgt. Ski." Now what was coincidental about Sgt. Ski is that we were both from Shreveport, LA. He gave me his home address, and after I got home, I went to see his folks to let them know that he was in a good place and was doing well. They were thankful for my visit. I have not seen Sgt. Ski since I left Vietnam.

I wrote a letter home on May 20 that had quite a bit of news about what was going on around Marble Mountain. First, I mentioned that it was getting really hot, and I was looking forward to getting home to Louisiana where it was only around ninety-five degrees. Well, that part was not very newsy. Everybody knows that it gets real, real hot in Southeast Asia in the summer! What made the letter newsworthy was the fact that I found out that I would not be home until the middle of August 1971. That news came to our company from Brigade Headquarters, and it was made known that there would be no more "drops" until Christmas. I reported in my letter that since I had been at Marble Mountain, I had seen many soldiers go home and about 95 percent of them got at least a twenty-day drop. There was probably more "hope" than "reality" in that statement. When I got down to the double digits of days left in-country, I really started paying attention every day as to how many days I had left. For example, in the letter of May 20, I made mention that I had eighty-three days left. When a soldier gets "short" on days left, the thoughts of home really become magnified. When a soldier gets down to the single digits, it is difficult to carry on a conversation about anything other than home!

Two months and three weeks left. Come on, globe . . . *spin*!

The globe continued to "spin" for me and many other soldiers, sailors, marines, and airmen. However, for the more than one thousand eight hundred American personnel that are still listed as POWs and MIAs by the United States Government, the globe has literally stopped. More than one thousand and eight hundred American fighters are still unaccounted for by the Department of Defense. It is my staunch belief that somebody, somewhere in North or South Vietnam, knows exactly where these men or their remains are located. It is also my belief that if these men are alive, they live in captivity, performing slave duty. One of those individuals is an American soldier who was assigned to the 282nd Assault Helicopter Company named Jerry Elliot. Jerry Elliot's sister, Donna, has been on the hunt for her brother for literally decades but has been unable to locate him or find signs that would convince her that her brother has deceased. I do not think Donna will ever stop her search to find her brother. And I contend that someone, somewhere, is aware of his location or the location of a burial plot which houses his remains. And once more, there are still more than one thousand eight hundred soldiers, marines, sailors, and airmen that our government cannot locate. It is indeed a sad fact that there are some of our servicemen who did not come home and whose time in this world has actually frozen. Hopefully, someday, their world will thaw, and time will start moving again for them.

CHAPTER ELEVEN

Hitching a Ride and Homeward Bound

June 1, 1971, found me counting days again until it was time for me to evacuate the country of South Vietnam. No matter which calendar I would use to count the days left in-country, they all figured to be the same . . . seventy-three days, seventy-three days, LXXIII days. With the passing of each day, though, I started the next with one less than I had the day before. I don't mean to insinuate that Vietnam was such a horrible place. I was just anxious to get home. Oh, now you want to know why I was so anxious to go home? Well, here it is: I missed my family, my friends, Momma's cooking, playing Rook with Daddy, and numerous other interests. Girls to chase? Oh yeah, I almost forgot about that one. There were girls to chase, pizza to eat, parties to attend, fish to be caught, hamburger cookouts, conditioned air to enjoy in the summer heat, cars to drive fast, and just several other amenities that South Vietnam did not offer a twenty-year-old soldier, returning from a year of combat duty. Vietnam was, however, a "horrible" place for the more than fifty-eight thousand families who lost a family member. And that number does not include the soldiers, sailors, marines, and airmen who were injured or rendered disabled by hostile acts. I was fortunate to spend my year in the combat zone and return home unscathed and unharmed. Oh, but I did create some vivid memories in that year on the other side of the world. Not only did my participation as a soldier in war create memories, my participation was also a teaching and a learning experience. I learned a lesson in life. I learned that life is not only "living" but that part of life is dying. Life should be lived in joy. I learned that liberty is very important to the quality of life. I learned that liberty is worth fighting for and that there is a price tag attached to liberty. Liberty is one of those things in life that is actually worth dying for. I learned that the pursuit of happiness is one of those liberties that enrich life. For one to have the pursuit of happiness, there has to have been someone or a collective force of people who put their lives at risk to provide for the pursuit of that happiness. Today, as Americans, we enjoy all three of the aforementioned. Many of our forefathers paid the ultimate price more than two hundred years ago, for us to enjoy life, liberty, and the pursuit of happiness. I am grateful to those forefathers, and I am thankful to be an American. I am willing to help others whose governing leaders forbid their subjects of these three inalienable rights.

As June 1970 came to an end, I had only forty-three days left in-country. Forty-three days! That was just a month and a half before I got to go home! Since I did not take an R & R, that meant that I would get to spend a whole month at home on leave before reporting for my next duty assignment. "R & R" is another government colloquialism, meaning to be on furlough to enjoy some time of rest and relaxation. Oh yes, I was ready. But to get there, I still had the entire month of July and the first part of August. Time was still marching on, and when it was my turn to go home, I'd be ready.

July 1971 roared right in with bad weather. After all, it was typhoon season in Southeast Asia. We kept flying our sorties as needed, and when the weather prohibited flying, we would roll as many helicopters into the hangars as possible. Usually, we had all the room we needed due to how we would place the ships that were required to be in the hangars.

Hello, July 4! Due to the fact that I only spent one July 4 in Vietnam, I was not privy to how all of the other July Fourths in Vietnam were spent. I am, however, sure of how Independence Day was celebrated in Vietnam by the 282nd Assault Helicopter Company in 1971. We celebrated the holiday with a P-A-R-T-Y! We were allowed to fly up to China Beach—yes, *that* China Beach—to have a cookout and a social gathering of GIs from the 282nd AHC. There were charcoal cookers fired up, and there were even adult beverages to enjoy. In Southeast Asia, during the summer months, the temperature can reach 130 degrees. So not all of our adult beverages were cold. That didn't matter too much to us though. If we had to drink warm beer, that's just what we did. China Beach is a beautiful beach spotted with some palm trees and plenty of sand to play in. Occasionally, there would be one of our helicopters that would fly in and land on the beach. Although I've never been mechanically sandblasted, I think I have a fairly good idea of how it would feel. When a UH-1 helicopter is hovering over a sandy beach, preparing to land, there is a tremendous displacement of sand that the prop wash from the rotors stirs up. If one happens to be in close proximity of a helicopter landing on a sandy beach, one will learn what it feels like to be sandblasted. But we just took it in stride because that ship might be bringing more goodies for our party, or it possibly could have some ice onboard to cool down some of the warm "brewskis" we were choking down. Yes, it was one of those memorable occurrences that I remember quite well when I think about my deployment to Vietnam.

The next letter that I wrote home was dated July 6, 1971. In this letter, I had commented on the fact that I had a new niece born to my next to the oldest brother, Ross, and his wife, Cathy. Of course, I wanted to know all about her—Shanon was her name—who she looked like, what color her eyes were, and things like that. I even asked if they had some pictures that they could send me, but I concurred that it would be all right if they didn't because I would be home to see her in just a few weeks anyway.

Also in the letter, I had told my brother Tommy about a rocket attack on DaNang Main that occurred recently. The *Stars and Stripes* newspaper had reported that it was the worst attack on DaNang Main for the year. I disagreed with that statement, though, because only one 122 mm rocket hit the base. The rocket made a direct hit on one of the marine barracks in "Gunfighter Village," killing three marines and injuring thirty-seven others. I ended this particular letter with congratulations to Ross and Cathy and said that I should be home in about thirty-six days.

As I began to think about preparing to go home, I had to decide what I needed to take home and what I could do without. Everything that I planned to take home had to fit into my duffel bag. A soldier's duffel bag is not a moving van. It is a heavy canvas bag that measures about four and a half feet tall and almost two feet in diameter. Everything that is packed in it must be pliable and flexible. A bookcase wouldn't work. So the things that I chose to pack up for my return trip home were primarily clothes, boots, sundry items, and any paperwork that I had to have with me at all times. At the time of my departure, I had twenty-one sets of jungle fatigues. I did not need that many jungle fatigues for stateside duty, so I think I packed two sets and left the rest with other GIs that might need them. That is precisely how I accumulated so many sets of fatigues. They were "hand-me-downs" from other soldiers who had gone home, so I passed them on to soldiers who were still deployed at Marble Mountain Air Facility after my own evacuation. I did not have room for all of the letters that I received while I was stationed in Vietnam. I did not want to throw them away due to the fact that they were personal letters that others had no reason to read, so I built a fire and burned them. This was tough to do. I am very close to my family, and burning letters from home is a heartbreaker. Again, I was limited to the amount of items that I could stuff into my duffel bag. I have wished many times that I would have left those two sets of jungle fatigues in Vietnam and packed my letters to bring home. I left my calendar on the wall for all to see as my time in-country began to dwindle in a serious manner. When July 12, 1971, rolled around, I positioned my "short-timer's ribbon" to the other side of my cap. This is the same ribbon that my brother Tommy had worn on his marine cap when his time in-country had been getting short. On the day of his departure, he had taken the ribbon off his cap and given it to me to put on my cap when my time was short. I wore it with pride.

On July 17, 1971, I wrote a letter home while I was on my lunch break. I had let Daddy know that I had received a letter from him and that I was "sorta looking for another one from you." It was right smack-dab in the middle of summer, and I was advising Daddy not to be outside cutting grass or any other energy-exerting odd jobs around the house because I knew that his leg and hip were not fully healed. Anyone who knew my daddy would know that those words would roll off his ears like water off a duck's back. Daddy had a passion for cutting grass, pulling weeds out of the flower beds, and anything else around the house that needed tending to, regardless of leg and hip pain. But I, at least, had to try to tell him to take it easy.

The very next day, July 18, I wrote another letter home. I had the afternoon off, and things around the base seemed to be pretty calm, and I guess I didn't have plans to do anything, so I decided to write a letter home. I remember the activity quite well because my tour was just about over, and our company was assigned two new AH-1 Cobra helicopters. The Cobras were at a base in Saigon, and one of the pilots that was assigned to fly one back to Marble Mountain was a good friend of mine, and he told me that if I could go with them to Saigon, he would let me fly back to Marble Mountain with him. In a new Cobra! I had ridden in a Mustang Cobra, built by Ford Motor Company, which had four tires, bucket seats, a big engine, but no rotors. The Cobras that our company was receiving, however, were built by Bell Helicopter Company. Big, big, huge difference from what the Ford folks were making. In 1971, the Bell AH-1 Cobra was the fiercest helicopter in the world.

Of course, for me to get to go to Saigon, I would have to obtain permission from the company commander. I asked him if I could go on the trip to retrieve the Cobras, and he told me that I would have to have orders from the battalion headquarters assigning me to the party that was assembled to go get the new Cobras. I did not have the orders to be assigned to the crew that would make that trip. Consequently, I did not get to go. Missing out on that opportunity just about broke my heart. It was just not to be, so I got over it and continued to do my duty.

I wrote only one more letter home in the month of July. In the letter of July 24, I had written that we were experiencing electrical problems at Marble Mountain. I had learned that the generators were just not putting out enough electricity to run the entire facility. So what did we do to get past that little "hiccup"? We did exactly what we were expected to do—we improvised and continued to do our duties. Things were a little difficult, but we made it through the days and nights just fine until the generators were able to produce the amount of electricity to sufficiently meet our needs. I can say with certainty that Charlie learned that a shortage of electricity would not keep our gunships on the ground. The gunships flew, the slicks flew, and the Cobras flew. What a force!

In the letter that I wrote on July 24, I asked my brother Tommy if he remembered when most of our company went to Dong Ha for temporary duty. I told him that when we went to Dong Ha, I remembered that his time was getting really short; in fact, Tommy had seventeen days left in-country. I was now experiencing the same feeling because on the day that I was writing this letter, I was down to eighteen days left in Vietnam. I told my family that, *I'm not home yet, but it won't be long.* In one of the recent letters that Momma had sent me, she told me that she would cook anything I wanted when I got home. Well, that was like opening the floodgates. I told her that I had thought about it, and the following is quoted directly from the letter of the twenty-fourth: *I want some homemade soup and a whole lot of cornbread. Then the next day, I want chicken and dumplings. Then some fried chicken, fried green tomatoes, fried okra, turnip greens, butter beans, and stuff like that. They say that when you first get home, your appetite is gone. Well, I don't believe it. I'd give $1,000.00 to eat some of the food I have listed now.* I was not taking a "cheap shot" at the food that our cooks were serving us in the mess hall—they did a good job. However, when you compare my momma's cooking to the food that we were being fed in the mess hall . . . well, you understand better why they call it the "mess hall."

I closed this letter with the following postscript: *Eighteen days left in Nam!*

The last letter that I have found that I wrote home from Vietnam was written on August 3, 1971. I had instructed my family that when they received this letter, they should not write to me anymore in Vietnam because I would miss them. There were a few days to spend processing out of the 282nd Assault Helicopter Company and a few days processing out of Cam Ranh Bay. I was scheduled to leave Marble Mountain on August 9, 1971, to go to Cam Ranh Bay, and I was scheduled to leave Cam Ranh Bay on Thursday, August 12, 1971. My destination? That would be Fort Lewis, Washington, United States of America!

Time passed, and on the morning of August 9, 1971, I boarded a C-130 Hercules at DaNang Main Air Base, also known as the Fifteenth Aerialport at DaNang. The trip to Cam Ranh Bay only took about two hours. I was in Cam Ranh Bay for about three days, and then, on August 12, I boarded a beautiful DC-8 jetliner, bound for Seattle, Washington, with a refueling stop at Yakota Base in Japan. The last time that I was in Japan (365 days ago), we were allowed to disembark the plane and walk around a bit. On the return trip, everybody stayed in their seats. We were quickly refueled and airborne again within about forty-five minutes, this time with the pilot entering the coordinates of Seattle, Washington, in the DC-8's array of cockpit instrumentation.

We completed the trip without incident, and the next ground surface that I put my feet on was my homeland. I arrived at Shreveport Regional Airport on August 12, 1971, to the open arms of my family. What a blessing! I thanked God for a successful tour, and I asked for Him to comfort the families who lost members in that stain of our country's history known as the Vietnam War.

Was my tour fun? No way, GI. Would I do it again, if needed? To use a quote from the former governor of Alaska, "You betcha!" I am profoundly proud of my American heritage, and I will be until my Lord calls me home.

Thank you for having interest in my story, and I hope you will join me in a collective statement to the rest of the entire world . . . "Don't tread on me. *Don't even think about it!*"

The End

CERTIFICATE OF APPRECIATION

FOR SERVICE IN THE ARMED FORCES OF THE UNITED STATES

JOSEPH HUGH RHODES   SPECIALIST FOUR   ARMY   27 JANUARY 70 - 13 JANUARY 72

I extend to you my personal thanks and the sincere appreciation of a grateful nation for your contribution of honorable service to our country. You have helped maintain the security of the nation during a critical time in its history with a devotion to duty and a spirit of sacrifice in keeping with the proud tradition of the military service.

I trust that in the coming years you will maintain an active interest in the Armed Forces and the purpose for which you served.

My best wishes to you for happiness and success in the future.

Richard Nixon

COMMANDER IN CHIEF

DEPARTMENT OF THE ARMY

CERTIFICATE OF APPRECIATION

In recognition of the active service of

JOSEPH HIGH RHODES   SPECIALIST FOUR   ARMY

The United States Army presents this testimonial
of esteem and gratitude for
Faithful Performance
of duty

W. C. Westmoreland
W. C. WESTMORELAND
General, United States Army
Chief of Staff

13 JANUARY 1972
DATE

Fly it

Mr. & Mrs. G.W. Rhodes
3802 Lakeshore Drive
Shreveport, La. 71103

SP/4 JOE RHODES
382nd Avi. Hel. Co.
APO SF 96349
Da Nang

- FREE -

FLY IT HOME

VIA AIR MAIL
CORREO AEREO
PAR AVION

MR. & MRS. GEORGE W. RHODES
3802 LAKESHORE DRIVE
SHREVEPORT, LA.   71109

JNK   FREE

FLY IT

MR. & MRS G.W. RHODES
3802 LAKESHORE DRIVE
SHREEVEPORT, LA. 71109

UNITED STATES ARMED FORCES · VIETNAM

SP/4 Joe Rhodes
282ND AHC
APO SF 96399

FLY IT HOME

FREE

VIA AIR MAIL
CORREO AEREO
PAR AVION

MR. & MRS. G.W. RHODES
3802 LAKESHORE DRIVE
SHREVEPORT, LA. 71109

SP14 JOE RHODES
282ND AHC
APO SF 96349

FLY IT HOME

FREE

VIA AIR MAIL
CORREO AEREO
PAR AVION

"60"

MR. & MRS. GEORGE W. RHODES
3802 LAKESHORE DRIVE
SHREVEPORT, LA. 71109

Calendar for year 1970 (United States)

January
Su	Mo	Tu	We	Th	Fr	Sa
				1	2	3
4	5	6	7	8	9	10
11	12	13	14	15	16	17
18	19	20	21	22	23	24
25	26	27	28	29	30	31

7:● 14:◑ 22:○ 30:◐

February
Su	Mo	Tu	We	Th	Fr	Sa
1	2	3	4	5	6	7
8	9	10	11	12	13	14
15	16	17	18	19	20	21
22	23	24	25	26	27	28

6:● 12:◑ 21:○ 28:◐

March
Su	Mo	Tu	We	Th	Fr	Sa
1	2	3	4	5	6	7
8	9	10	11	12	13	14
15	16	17	18	19	20	21
22	23	24	25	26	27	28
29	30	31				

7:● 14:◑ 22:○ 30:◐

April
Su	Mo	Tu	We	Th	Fr	Sa
			1	2	3	4
5	6	7	8	9	10	11
12	13	14	15	16	17	18
19	20	21	22	23	24	25
26	27	28	29	30		

5:● 13:◑ 21:○ 28:◐

May
Su	Mo	Tu	We	Th	Fr	Sa
					1	2
3	4	5	6	7	8	9
10	11	12	13	14	15	16
17	18	19	20	21	22	23
24	25	26	27	28	29	30
31						

5:● 13:◑ 20:○ 27:◐

June
Su	Mo	Tu	We	Th	Fr	Sa
	1	2	3	4	5	6
7	8	9	10	11	12	13
14	15	16	17	18	19	20
21	22	23	24	25	26	27
28	29	30				

3:● 12:◑ 19:○ 26:◐

July
Su	Mo	Tu	We	Th	Fr	Sa
			1	2	3	4
5	6	7	8	9	10	11
12	13	14	15	16	17	18
19	20	21	22	23	24	25
26	27	28	29	30	31	

3:● 11:◑ 18:○ 25:◐

August
Su	Mo	Tu	We	Th	Fr	Sa
						1
2	3	4	5	6	7	8
9	10	11	12	13	14	15
16	17	18	19	20	21	22
23	24	25	26	27	28	29
30	31					

2:● 10:◑ 16:○ 23:◐ 31:●

September
Su	Mo	Tu	We	Th	Fr	Sa
		1	2	3	4	5
6	7	8	9	10	11	12
13	14	15	16	17	18	19
20	21	22	23	24	25	26
27	28	29	30			

8:◑ 15:○ 22:◐ 30:●

October
Su	Mo	Tu	We	Th	Fr	Sa
				1	2	3
4	5	6	7	8	9	10
11	12	13	14	15	16	17
18	19	20	21	22	23	24
25	26	27	28	29	30	31

8:◑ 14:○ 21:◐ 30:●

November
Su	Mo	Tu	We	Th	Fr	Sa
1	2	3	4	5	6	7
8	9	10	11	12	13	14
15	16	17	18	19	20	21
22	23	24	25	26	27	28
29	30					

6:◑ 13:○ 20:◐ 28:●

December
Su	Mo	Tu	We	Th	Fr	Sa
		1	2	3	4	5
6	7	8	9	10	11	12
13	14	15	16	17	18	19
20	21	22	23	24	25	26
27	28	29	30	31		

5:◑ 12:○ 20:◐ 28:●

Holidays and Observances:

Jan 1 New Year's Day	Jun 21 Father's Day	Nov 3 Election Day
Feb 12 Lincoln's Birthday	Jul 3 'Independence Day' observed	Nov 11 Veterans Day
Feb 14 Valentine's Day	Jul 4 Independence Day	Nov 26 Thanksgiving Day
Mar 29 Easter Sunday	Sep 7 Labor Day	Dec 24 Christmas Eve
May 10 Mother's Day	Oct 12 Columbus Day (Most regions)	Dec 25 Christmas Day
May 30 Memorial Day	Oct 31 Halloween	

17 JULY 1970

STATEMENT

I JOSEPH H RHODES Company A 2nd TSBDE USATSCH (2120) Ft Eustis, Virginia 23604 hereby waive my choice of remaining in CONUS in favor of assignment to Vietnam. Coercion has not been used to obtain this statement from me.

M°M° MICHAEL
2 LT WAC
Asst Adjutant

JOSEPH H° RHODES
PV2

III. APPLICABLE ONLY TO ENLISTED PERSONNEL; OFFICERS IN THE GRADE OF LIEUTENANT
COLONEL (O5) OR BELOW; AND PERSONNEL WHO INDICATE "NO" IN PART I:

A. I UNDERSTAND THAT: 1. If I am slightly wounded or injured as a result
of hostile action, I may elect not to have my next of kin notified of my wound or
injury; 2. The term "slightly wounded" is defined as a wound or injury sustained
as a result of hostile action which medical authorities do not consider as being
seriously wounded or injured endangering life; 3. If the slight wound or injury
precludes my being able to communicate with my next of kin this election is void.

√ B. With the above understanding, I elect that my next of kin:
_____ not be notified _____ be notified.

C. I further understand that this election is not binding and that I may
change it at any time.

Joseph H. Rhodes   18 AUG 1970
(Signature)   (Date)

IV. APPLICABLE TO ALL PERSONNEL:

A. I have reviewed my Record of Emergency Data (DA Form 41) and find the
information concerning my next of kin to be correct.

B. Unless otherwise indicated on my record of Emergency Data, there is no
known physical ailment or mental condition that would make notification of my next
of kin unwise.

Joseph H. Rhodes   18 AUG 1970
(Signature)   (Date)

III. APPLICABLE ONLY TO ENLISTED PERSONNEL;OFFICERS IN THE GRADE OF LIEUTENANT COLONEL (05) OR BELOW; AND PERSONNEL WHO INDICATE "NO" IN PART I:

    A. I UNDERSTAND THAT: 1. If I am slightly wounded or injured as a result of hostile action, I may elect not to have my next of kin notified of my wound or injury; 2. The term "slightly wounded" is defined as a wound or injury sustained as a result of hostile action which medical authorities do not consider as being seriously wounded or injured endangering life; 3. If the slight wound or injury precludes my being able to communicate with my next of kin this election is void.

    B. With the above understanding, I elect that my next of kin:
_____ not be notified _____ be notified.

    C. I further understand that this election is not binding and that I may change it at any time.

                                         Joseph H. Blades _18 AUG 1970_
                                           (Signature)   (Date)

IV. APPLICABLE TO ALL PERSONNEL:

    A. I have reviewed my Record of Emergency Data (DA Form 41) and find the information concerning my next of kin to be correct.

    B. Unless otherwise indicated on my record of Emergency Data, there is no known physical ailment or mental condition that would make notification of my next of kin unwise.

                                         Joseph H. Blades _18 Aug. 1970_
                                         (Signature)   (Date)

25, APR. 70

Dear Folks,

Well, it sure was good to hear from home tonight. I hate that you all didn't get that letter that I mailed Tuesday. Oh yea, I didn't give you my complete address over the phone tonight either. I left a set of numbers out. I'll write the correct one on the back of this sheet. Send me Tommy's address in your next letter also. I'm glad to hear that he is doing alright now. I'm sure he'll make it O.K.

Fred, I'll be ~~the~~ authorized to wear a set of wings when I graduate. Actually it's the crewmembers badge. They're really better looking than the regular pilots wings to me. But, I'm not gonna stop at crewmembers badge. I'll get those pilots wings if there's anyway possible.

School is getting pretty involved now. My easiest class is just about the hardest for the rest of the students that I'm with. The only reason for that is that I've had it before at Tech.

It's "Principles of Flight." We even have to learn stuff like that. The more of that kind of stuff I learn will help me more in flight school. We made our first project yesterday. They gave us a piece of helicopter metal that had bullet holes in them. We had to cut out the damaged portions and re-cover the sheets. It was pretty interesting. I think I'll like it OK.

It's pretty quiet around here tonight. Everyone has gone on pass. I had one, but I'm kinda broke so I chose to stay here. I felt sorta constructive tonight, so I painted 12 wall lockers. Now everything in our bay is perfect. The company knows that Bay 10 is the sharpest bay in the company. The CO & XO even talk about it. It makes us feel good when we hear the commander talk about Bay 10 in front of a company formation.

Well, I guess I'd better go for now. So write when you can. I'll do the same.

Love
Joe

11 June '71

Dear Folks,

Well, how is everything at home?
Fine I hope.

Things are a little more "newsy"
around here than last I wrote.
Yesterday, one of our helicopters
went down. It had a power failure
at about 150 feet while it was at
a hover lowering supplies. Nobody
was hurt, but it's only a wonder.
The ship was totally demolished.

Then, this evening, we had a foot
and wall locker inspection!! That really
made some people mad. A regular
personnel inspection is bad enough for
Nam, much less a blasted foot &
wall locker inspection. That's really
about all that's happened around
here.

Tommy, I've been getting a little
"skate time" in lately. It's
really nice to be able to walk
across the runway and on to the
beach. You should see marine
side now. No marine ships
at all. There are just a
few left on this compound.
I think half of the marines
are on zulu guard, so that

tells you about how many marines we have left here. I haven't gotten back to Mag-11 since you left. They wouldn't give me a pass to go over and then when Da Nang went "on limits" I would have to get my C.O. or the battalion X.O. to sign me a pass. So as I'm sure you understand, I've not seen Dixon.

Has Paul left yet? I hope I get home before he leaves. I still don't know where I'll go when I leave here. Maybe Germany. Then maybe Ft. Head. I'm hoping for Head.

It looks like they're going to make me spend the entire 365 days here. I've got 61 left now. Someday, not too long from now, I'll be able to walk around telling everyone I'm definitely SHORT!

Mama, did you get the pictures I sent you in my last letter? I spect you did.

Well, I guess I'd better go for now. It's getting pretty late and I'd better go on to sleep. Write when you can and take care of yourselves. Daddy, why don't you drop me a line.

Love
Joe

29 June '71

Dear Folks,

How are things at home? All is about the same around here. Sorry I haven't written in so long. I think the last time I wrote was 10 days ago. I could have written, but things have been pretty bad around here lately. We had an I.G. inspection a few days ago and the C.O. & 1st Sgt. were all afraid we wouldn't pass it, but we scored "excellent" in all areas. I was surprised they didn't make us wax the hangar floor for it.

Mama, you asked me to tell you about the drug problem here. Well, it is bad. The Army is really beginning to crack down on it now and I believe it's doing a lot of good. They're making all returning G.I.'s take tests for it. I think it's mainly just a urine test, but if a person is on drugs, it'll show it. A lot of G.I.'s got scared and turned themselves in on the Drug Amnesty Program. If you're caught using drugs, you don't get to go home. They keep you here for 3 weeks and then send you to some place in California for rehabilitation I think. There's a lot of guys that won't get to go home. But I can gladly say, I'll be home with bells on.

I saw in the paper today that they're getting sorta rough at that Rock festival in McCrea. I don't know why anyone would want to go to something like that. I guess people will wake up someday though.

I guess you heard about Fire Base Fuller getting overrun the other day. Don't let that bother any of you, because it's not as bad as it's publicized. And you need not worry about Marble Mountain getting overrun either, because there's no way they could do it without bringing the whole NVA in here. We might get a few rockets and mortars and possibly even a small ground attack, but that's about it. Rockets and mortars will be going for helicopters and the ground attack probably wouldn't get passed the perimeter wire. I'm not sweating it.

Well, I guess I'd better close this and get it in the mail. I'll start writing more often. I've said that before, but I'll try anyway. Write when you can and take care of yourselves.

Love
Joe

P.S.
43 DAYS UNTIL

HOME

3 Aug. '71

Dear Folks,

Well, how are things at home? All
is about the same around here I guess.
Well, when this letter gets home, don't write
anymore to me here because I'd miss them.
I'm leaving Da Nang the 9th to go to Cam Ranh
Bay to process out. I'll leave Cam Ranh the
12th and go to Ft. Lewis, Washington via Japan
and Alaska I think. I'll leave here the 12th,
but it'll be the 11th in the states. So, I'll
arrive in the states on the 12th I don't know
how long they'll keep me in Washington, or
I don't know for sure when I'll be in S'port.
I've heard they'll keep me in Washington for only
about 6 hours, but you know how the Army is.
I might be there for 3 days. I'm kinda banking
on the 6 hour rumor though. If that's true,
I'll be home late at night on the 12th or early
the 13th. That's gonna be 1 long day, but a happy one.

I don't have to work anymore. I just sorta
lay around and read or play chess or something.
I've got a pretty bad throat now. It started
scratching 3 days ago but it's gotten better.
I surely hope I don't have it when I come home.

Well, I guess I'll go for now. I'll write
a couple of more times before I leave and probably
once from Cam Ranh Bay. So, tell everyone
I'll see them in a few days. (About 2) Take care
of yourselves. Love
          Joe

18 July '71

Dear Folks,

Well, how are things at home? Fine I hope. I'm alright I guess. I have this afternoon off and decided to drop a few lines.

There's not much going on around here. It's a pretty quiet day. I thought I was going to get to go to Saigon this weekend, but the CO wouldn't let me. He said I'd have to have orders to go. Anyway, my company is going to get 2 Cobra helicopter gun ships and they're in Saigon. One Cobra pilot, a friend of mine, said I could fly back with him in the Cobra, but the CO wouldn't let me. It really made me sick. Oh well —

Well I'm going to be coming home pretty soon I guess. I've got about 24 days left in country, so I should be home around the 15th of next month. I'm still not sure whether I'm going to Europe from here or not. I don't think a tour of Germany would be too bad.

Well, this is short, but there's just no news. So, I guess I'll go and get this in the mail. Write when you can and take care of yourselves. See you all in about 26 days —

Love
Roy